men 12

THE ACADEMIC COMMUNITY

An Essay on Organization

An Essay on Organization

The Academic
Community

John D. Millett
President, Miami University, Oxford, Ohio

McGraw-Hill Book Company, Inc.   1962
New York   San Francisco   Toronto   London

THE ACADEMIC COMMUNITY

42266

TO
MY
COLLEAGUES

in the
Exciting Enterprise
of
Higher Education

Preface

I MUST BLAME this little volume upon two of my colleagues on the Board of Trustees of the Institute for College and University Administrators. One challenged me at a meeting with these words: "I have read all the literature on public administration in order to find some light on the problems of administration in higher education, and I have failed to find anything helpful." He then asked me directly: "Is there anything in the study of public administration which can assist those of us engaged in research and teaching on the subject of higher education?"

As a political scientist and as a one-time professor of public administration, here was a challenge I could scarcely ignore. I had to admit that political science as a discipline had given slight attention to higher education as an activity of the state. There was little in the writing on government in this country to illuminate the operation of our colleges and universities. The one recent exception came about almost entirely because of a Ford Foundation grant which did enable two political scientists of the Johns Hopkins University to inquire specifically into the relationships of state government to state-supported colleges and universities. In the writing on organization and management, scholars of public administration have never seen fit to look at the peculiar characteristics of higher education, even in its public setting.

As I pondered these facts, I could not avoid the question whether there was something special and distinctive which should be said about the internal organizational structure of a university. The more I considered this issue, the more convinced I became that there was something distinctive to say and that I ought to try to say it.

This wondering on my part led me to remark on occasion to another one of my fellow trustees that I felt it was time for me to write a little essay on university organization and administration. All the encouragement or sympathy I received was a caustic comment: "Well, it's about time!" I wasn't certain whether he thought I ought to write before the hands of fate caught up with me and I was no longer a university administrative officer, or whether he thought I had better demonstrate that an administrative officer could still write. The only answer seemed to be to sit down and put a few words together.

I first began to ponder the issues outlined here when as a political scientist I was asked to direct the research program of the Commission on Financing Higher Education, sponsored by the Association of American Universities under grants from the Rockefeller Foundation and the Carnegie Corporation. In my studies between 1949 and 1952, I developed not only a growing appreciation for higher education as an institution in this country but I began to perceive something of the necessary difference between higher education and other institutions of our social life.

As chief administrative officer of a state-supported university, and as a participant in educational and other conferences throughout the United States, I have become increasingly convinced that higher education as an institution must be presented in its own light and understood in terms of its own peculiar function of intellectual enlightenment. And it is in these terms that it must be studied as an organizational entity. It is this which I have endeavored to do herein.

I am, of course, indebted to many friends, colleagues, and acquaintances in and outside our colleges and universities for their stimulating conversations. No man is ever an island, intellectually or socially. Much of what I have to say I have heard others say more dramatically and more incisively.

I am particularly grateful to several personal friends for reading and criticizing the manuscript: Dr. Dexter Keezer, economic consultant to the McGraw-Hill Publishing Company; Prof. T. R. McConnell, chairman of the Center for the Study of Higher Education at the University of California (Berkeley); Prof. Ferrel Heady, director of the Institute of Public Administration of the University of Michigan; and Dr. F. Glenn Macomber, formerly a dean at Miami University and in 1961–1962 a visiting professor of higher education at Southern Illinois University. I wish especially to express my appreciation for assistance given by Prof. Algo D. Henderson, director of the Center for the Study of Higher Education at the University of Michigan.

My friends in the McGraw-Hill Book Company have been most encouraging and helpful, as always. And I owe thanks to three young women in my office who at different times have had the chore of typing and retyping the manuscript: Mrs. Janice K. Wilkinson, Mrs. Kay S. Irwin, and Mrs. Janet W. Hurley.

John D. Millett

Contents

xi

Chapter 1

Organization
and Higher Education

AMERICANS HAVE a great interest in organization. Most of us carry on our productive endeavors in some kind of formal aggregation of various persons. Specialization of activity is a way of life. In unity of individual effort we have found social strength. Increased productivity and group cohesion are widely accepted as desirable results of our organizational practice. A leading economist has written about "the organizational revolution," [1] and an observant journalist has recorded the salient characteristics of "the organization man." [2]

American scholars of social science—especially those in the disciplines of economics, political science, sociology, and social psychology—appear to be

[1] Kenneth E. Boulding, *The Organizational Revolution* (New York: Harper & Brothers, 1953).
[2] William H. Whyte, Jr., *The Organization Man* (New York: Simon and Schuster, Inc., 1956).

1

giving increasing attention to the structural and behavioral aspects of organized activity. Faculty members in various professions, such as public school education, public health, military affairs, social welfare,
business affairs, and public management, are more
and more concerned to observe and pass along the
wisdom of experience in organized endeavor.

This particular concern with the structure,
process, and performance of man in formal aggregations of activity has not overlooked the institution of
higher education in our society. In the aftermath of
World War II, with the deluge of veterans and then
a brief period of declining enrollments, with ever-
growing concern about the financing of higher education, many colleges and universities were encouraged
to retain management consultants to study how to promote operating efficiency. Other colleges and universities began self-studies. Numerous articles and some
books began to discuss the organizational features of
the individual colleges and universities which make
up the American institution of higher education.

It is not too much to say that organizational life
has become a major preoccupation of intellectual as
well as practical concern in American society today.
It is altogether natural that this should be the case.
Not only do most of us work in organizations. Our
economic output, our public service, our academic
achievement depend upon the successful performance
of organizations. More than this, our leadership
among Western nations and among opponents of
Communist domination rests upon organizational
accomplishment. Indeed, organization has become a

matter of urgent personal and social survival. There can be no social progress which is not founded upon the ever-improving output of organized units of group endeavor. There can be no knowledge of social institutions and of social process which is not founded upon a science and art of organization.

All this concern, not just with higher education but also with economic production and public service, has revealed only too clearly how little we know about organization. Political scientists have been studying public administration for more than seventy years in the United States. Engineers and business managers, together with those who teach engineering and business administration, have been studying the organization of the productive process and of the company for the same length of time. As a young professor at Bryn Mawr, Woodrow Wilson wrote the first important essay on "the study of administration" in 1887. Frederick W. Taylor had pioneered his techniques of "scientific management" by 1886, and in that year Henry R. Towne presented his paper on "the engineer as economist" before the newly organized American Society of Mechanical Engineers. Yet in all the years since these beginnings, our practice has far outrun our theory or science. The art of organization has much more to its credit in our country than has the science of organization.

As a political scientist myself, and as a political scientist with a special interest in public administration, I am of course more conversant with the literature and thought concerning the public service than I am with the literature and thought on business management. Yet I have had occasion to read a number of books about organization of the business corporation written by both business managers and professors of business administration. Personal experience has given me substantial contact with able business executives as well as with competent management consultants. I believe I know something about the prevailing thinking in business management even as in public administration.

It is not my concern here to write a treatise about concepts of business or governmental administration. I am interested in the impact which thinking drawn largely from business and public management has had upon an understanding of the organizational structure of American colleges and universities. I can state my thesis in a few words: *I believe ideas drawn from business and public administration have only a very limited applicability to colleges and universities.* More than this, the essential ideas about business and public administration, such as they are, may actually promote a widespread and unfortunate misunderstanding of the nature of the college and university in our society.

In this discussion I shall refer to higher education as a social institution comparable in concept to the family, the church, the economy, the voluntary group, and the government as institutions of our society. I shall avoid use of the word "institutions" as a synonym for individual colleges and universities. From necessity I must utilize the cumbersome phrase "colleges and universities" in referring to the many different entities which perform the tasks of higher education and which constitute the institution of higher education.

Nor is it relevant to the present discussion to dwell upon the real and imagined differences which distinguish a college from a university. There are differences to some extent in size of enrollment, scope of educational activity, and degree of internal complexity which separate a university from a college, but these are not of primary importance to me here.

There are many other differences among colleges and universities which in another context would require some attention. There are differences in type of program (the junior or community college as distinct from the separate liberal arts college), in relationship to religious denominations (the church-related college or university as distinct from the independent college or university), in the nature of the sponsorship (private as distinct from public), and in location (the urban, locally oriented college or university as distinct from the small-town or non-locally oriented and residential college or university). These are all differences of great importance in particular discussions of higher education in the United States. Nonetheless, they are only of incidental and passing interest here.

There is another introductory qualification which I must make explicit. I am concerned to explore certain aspects of the internal structure and process of a college or university. I am not particularly concerned with the relationships of the publicly sponsored college and university to the legislative, executive, or judicial branches of government, or to central administrative control agencies. I am not particularly concerned with the relationships of colleges and universities to the various interest groups and business and public enterprises which operate within our society. Attention here is directed to the internal functioning of colleges and universities.

With these explanations out of the way, let us examine certain aspects of this subject of the relationship of knowledge about organization, both theoretical and practical, to the operating units, the colleges and universities, of our institution of higher education.

The Source of Organizational Knowledge

The first major observation to be made is that ideas about organizations have been drawn mostly from two particular types of group activity: the business enterprise and the governmental administrative agency. To be sure, there is great variety among business enterprises and administrative agencies. There are individual, partnership, and corporate forms of business; there are productive enterprises (farming, mining, and manufacturing) and service enterprises (from beauty parlors and radio repair shops to finance and banking, transportation, communication, and amusement or recreation services); there are local businesses and great national and international businesses; there are integrated businesses (from mining and manufacturing to distribution) and businesses which specialize in parts of the process of production and distribution of goods.

Similarly, among governmental administrative agencies there are those which represent an institutionalizing of legislative, executive, or judicial power in government; there are those which perform some centralized "housekeeping" services, such as the construction of buildings or the purchase and distribution of supplies; there are so-called "operating" agencies which may be labeled "executive departments" or "independent agencies" (apart from an executive department);[3] there are regulatory boards and commissions and government corporations; there are peculiar governmental and administrative combinations, such as the local school district; there are interstate compact agencies, such as the Port of New York Authority; and I might even add as still another distinct category that there are publicly sponsored colleges and universities.

There are substantial differences indeed among these various kinds of business and governmental enterprises. Yet the literature in business and public administration for the most part gives little if any attention to these differences. Rather, much of the literature and thinking on business administration seems to picture an ideal structure and process for

[3] Since the National Security Act amendments of 1949, there have existed in the federal government three "military departments" as components of the executive Department of Defense.

the operation of a large manufacturing corporation with nationwide interests. Similarly, much of the literature and thinking about public administration seems to picture an ideal structure and process for the operation of a large executive department, usually in the federal government. The great variety and diversity of business and governmental activities are often lost in the attempt to provide elements of common experience or desirable practice with general applicability.

There are those who suggest that the administrative process is essentially similar, whether it be concerned with foreign relations, national defense, hospital management and patient care, religious affairs, business enterprise, or education. I shall have more to say shortly about the German sociologist, Max Weber, whose influence has been so great upon the thinking and writing of American scholars in the social sciences. In his characterization of bureaucracy, Weber found common features in such diverse institutional settings as business, government, and the church.[4] More recently, Edward H. Litchfield has declared: "Administration and the administrative process occur in substantially the same generalized form in industrial, commercial, civil, educational, military, and hospital organizations." [5]

[4] See H. H. Gerth and C. Wright Mills, *From Max Weber: Essays in Sociology* (London: Kegan Paul, Trench, Trubner & Co., 1947), chap. VII.

[5] Edward H. Litchfield, "Notes on a General Theory of Administration," *Administrative Science Quarterly,* vol. 1 (June, 1956), p. 28.

I would like to point out that there is very little empirical evidence to sustain the thesis or hypothesis that organizational forms are similar or that bureaucracies necessarily behave in similar patterns regardless of the institutional setting. And while similar problems of organization are to be observed in varied fields of activity, there is little empirical evidence to suggest that solutions which appear by some set of criteria to be satisfactory in one kind of business enterprise or governmental agency will necessarily be equally satisfactory by the same set of criteria for a different kind of enterprise or agency.

In any event, I wish to assert no more at the moment than that much of the thinking about organization has been extracted from the institutional context of business and public service and that even here little attention has been given to the variety of types of endeavor which actually exist in the economy or in the administrative activity of government.

Structural Theory

In general, two points of view or two analytical approaches have been developed in an effort to formulate a theory of organization. One of these we may label the "formal" or "structural" theory of organization. The other may be called a "behavioral" theory of organization. Some enthusiasts believe that only one or the other theory is sensible, logical, or scientific, but it seems to me that both points of view are today useful in understanding organization.[6] It appears to me that the two are complementary rather than competing, and that to utilize one to the exclusion of the other is to limit our understanding of organization.

It must be said at the outset, I believe, that our theories of organization, both structural and behavioral, are partial and sketchy. Our knowledge about organizational life in society is far from being complete or comprehensive. Our practice of management has far outrun our actual knowledge as such.

On occasion scholars of public administration and professors or practitioners of business administration have attempted to construct certain rules of thumb for the guidance of organizational arrangements. They have spoken of such factors as the functional grouping of related activities, unity of command, span of control, line and staff, work simplification, work measurement, and coordination. When these and other rules have been subjected to critical analysis, and when efforts have been made to establish clear standards of empirical evidence with which to evaluate various organizational practices, these ideas have not fared too well.[7] It appears that

[6] The idea of two types of theory about organization has been recognized by various scholars but not made so explicit as actual development would seem to warrant. See, for example, James G. March and Herbert A. Simon, *Organizations* (New York: John Wiley & Sons, Inc., 1958); and Ferrel Heady, "Bureaucratic Theory and Comparative Administration," *Administrative Science Quarterly,* vol. 4 (March, 1959), p. 509.

[7] In the study of public administration the critical assessment of prevailing ideas in organization will be found, among other places, in Schuyler C. Wallace, *Federal Departmentaliza-*

the ideas about organization in business administration have been less critically examined than those in public administration. Yet even here there has been some indication of a growing sophistication, and caution, in discussing organizational problems.

Structural theory as it has emerged over the years sets forth certain basic elements of organizational practice as it has been observed in governmental and business administration.[8] The fundamental propositions which have emerged are relatively few and simple. I would summarize them in this way.

1. Organization is purposive, designed to bring together a number and variety of persons who working with one another undertake to accomplish a defined purpose (a product or service).

---

tion: *A Critique of Theories of Organization* (New York: Columbia University Press, 1941); and in Dwight Waldo, *The Administrative State: A Study of the Political Theory of American Public Administration* (New York: The Ronald Press Company, 1948).

[8] The most systematic attempt to set forth a structural theory of organization by a political scientist is that by Luther Gulick, "Notes on the Theory of Organization," in Luther Gulick and L. Urwick, eds., *Papers on the Science of Administration* (New York: Institute of Public Administration, 1937), p. 1. A recent effort at both system and synthesis in organizational theory is that of John M. Pfiffner and Frank P. Sherwood, *Administrative Organization* (Englewood Cliffs, N.J.: Prentice-Hall, Inc., 1960). There are many volumes which treat concepts of business organization from a structural point of view. It seems to me that these are representative: Paul E. Holden, Lounsbury S. Fish, and Hubert L. Smith, *Top-management Organization and Control* (Stanford, Calif.: Stanford University Press, 1941); L. Urwick, *The Elements of Adminis-*

2. Organization is built upon the basis of individual and group specialization, individuals and aggregations of individuals contributing a particular skill or process to the realization of the desired purpose.

3. Organization requires integration of specialized efforts, in order that the least possible input of personnel, plant, materials, and other resources may be utilized in accomplishing the desired output.

4. Organization provides a structure of leadership in which techniques of planning, direction, and supervision communicate a sense of shared purpose, build a common objective and allegiance, and recognize achievement.

Perhaps four such statements suggest an impoverished theory. As with many propositions in the social sciences, these embrace elements of common sense as well as empirical observation. In the social sciences, we cannot often experiment at will with organizational arrangements. People working in an organization are human beings, and they cannot ordinarily be moved around to satisfy the needs of a scientist seeking to discover laws or principles of predictable behavior.

---

tration (New York: Harper & Brothers, 1943); Alvin Brown, *Organization: A Formulation of Principle* (New York: Hibbert Printing Co., 1945); Ralph Currier Davis, *The Fundamentals of Top Management* (New York: Harper & Brothers, 1951). For an indication of growing dissatisfaction with these structural ideas in the teaching of business administration, see Charles E. Summer, Jr., *Factors in Effective Administration* (New York: Graduate School of Business, Columbia University, 1956).

Occasionally, there are recognized failures in organizational performance, and sometimes the pathological evidence can be isolated and identified. In this way we learn something about organization. There is also change in organizational practices under the pressure of outstanding leadership, changing circumstances, and other forces. We learn from these situations too. Furthermore, a comparison of organizational arrangements among governmental agencies and business enterprises broadens our understanding and sometimes even suggests preferable arrangements. I would be among the first to say that this gradual accumulation of observation and experience is still far short of a science of organization.

Sociologists interested in organization have tended to stress the importance of the purposive or goal-oriented factor in organizational structure and process. Talcott Parsons identifies "primacy of orientation to the attainment of a specific goal" as the distinguishing characteristic of organization.[9] Sociologists and psychologists have also been much interested in the importance of leadership which accepts the responsibility for providing direction to an enterprise and for promoting a common purpose. Philip Selznick has emphasized in particular the vital role of leadership in an organizational structure, observing that

[9] Talcott Parsons, *Structure and Process in Modern Societies* (Glencoe, Ill.: Free Press, 1960), p. 17. The first two essays in this collection of papers are entitled "A Sociological Approach to the Theory of Organizations" and "A General Theory of Organization."

the first duty of administrative leadership is to define the mission and goals for organizational accomplishment.[10]

The interrelationship between purpose and organizational structure has not been easy to define. That there is a vital connection seems apparent. How one influences the other has not been carefully explored. Here it seems to me is one of the important gaps in our organizational theory.

It is clearly evident that organization is built upon specialization of effort. Formal organization of a productive or service enterprise comes about when several persons combine their efforts or their diverse talents in a common cause. The basis of such division of labor has not been clearly stated in theoretical terms. We know that technology, skill, process, and purpose all have something to do with specialization of endeavor. Just how each of these factors operates in any particular situation, and whether these factors suggest a common pattern of endeavor, we do not know.

It seems to me that there are obviously four broad categories of skills which must be brought together in a large, modern organizational structure. These groups may be labeled "operators," "supervisors," "specialists or technical advisers," and "managers." We cannot pause here to develop this idea of varied groups in the structural division of labor. The idea itself needs much exploration and refinement. I am not certain whether it is possible to describe di-

[10] Philip Selznick, *Leadership in Administration* (Evanston, Ill.: Row, Peterson & Company, 1957).

vision of labor in any more exact terms and still have elements of common experience in many different types of endeavor.

The concept of integration is one of common sense and observation. Specialized efforts in a common purpose need a common relationship. It has been pointed out by Gulick and others that integration may be sought in terms of a function or particular product, in terms of common service in a geographical area, in terms of varied services to a particular clientele, or in terms of some common process, such as the construction of buildings. It is not easy to differentiate function from process, and definition of clientele may be difficult to distinguish from a geographical area of operation.

Moreover, integration of effort may be simple or complex. March and Simon have contributed an important observation about organizational structure by making a distinction between "unitary" and "federal" organization.[11] They define an organization as unitary if the scope of total activity coincides with a means-end structure involving a single "operational" goal. A goal is operational if there are criteria for determining the contribution of each subprogram (organizational specialization) to the accomplishment of a specific, concretely defined objective. An organization is federal if it brings together a number of different unitary operations. The production of a single type or kind of automobile would involve a unitary operation. The production of several different types of automobiles, along with refrigerators, aircraft en-

[11] March and Simon, *op. cit.*, p. 195.

gines, and other items would involve a federal structure of organization.

There are thus different bases of integration of activity in a particular organizational entity, and there may be a varied scope or extent of integration in a particular organizational entity, whether governmental or business.

A great many more details of organization might be discussed here, together with various examples of different kinds of experience. I desire to do no more than simply outline the basic dimensions of a structural theory of organization in so far as these can be identified from a wide variety of governmental administrative agencies and business units. I am reluctant to suggest that our current knowledge goes much farther in finding elements of common experience or in suggesting that one structural pattern of operation is clearly superior to another. The pattern of integration in an organization may require adjustment from time to time, but the prescription of a desirable and different pattern is much more an art of leadership than a matter of validated science.

Behavioral Theory

Two major criticisms have been directed against a structural theory of organization as just sketched by those who favor the behavioral approach. First, it is asserted that structural theory provides very little in the way of knowledge or guidelines to action in the construction of organizational arrangements for people working together, and even less help in the solution of felt or identified organizational difficulties. Such observations as have been made about organizational structure, it is said, constitute broad common-sense generalizations, and where more exact maxims are offered these turn out to be the judgment of an individual rarely if ever subject to empirical validation from experimentation or extensive observation. Secondly, we are told that organizational structure is a figment of the imagination anyway. Actually, these critics tell us, organization is a pattern of behavior by the persons and groups of persons who make up an administrative identity. It is only this pattern of behavior which has any reality.[12]

I am tempted to remark that the advocates of a behavioral approach to organization have been more

[12] The first great book setting forth the behavioral approach to organization was written by the president of the New Jersey Bell Telephone Company of the American Telephone and Telegraph System, who was later president of the Rockefeller Foundation, Chester I. Barnard, *The Functions of the Executive* (Cambridge, Mass.: Harvard University Press, 1938). Actually, studies undertaken during the 1930s under the direction of Prof. Elton Mayo of the Harvard Graduate School of Business Administration had launched a growing concern with the personal and behavioral aspects of organization. Perhaps the best known of these studies, the Hawthorne experiments, is that of F. J. Roethlisberger and W. J. Dickson, *Management and the Worker* (Cambridge, Mass.: Harvard University Press, 1939). For a general summary of these studies see Elton Mayo, *The Social Problems of an Industrial Civilization* (Boston: Division of Research, Graduate School of Business Administration, Harvard University, 1945).

interested in criticizing the structural theorists than in constructing propositions of their own.[13] Certainly the criticisms have been convincing and have made structural theorists more cautious in their claims to an exact knowledge. In this the criticism has had a useful result. The behavioral theorists have also added a new dimension to our understanding of organization. They have made everyone aware of the human element in organization.

It is not easy to go beyond this, however, and to set forth basic propositions to which the behavioral theorist subscribes. From a study of the literature in the field, I would suggest that there are certain fundamental ideas which the behavioral theorists have undertaken to develop.[14] I would endeavor to summarize these as follows.

1. Organization involves elements of work specialization and of integration that are to be observed primarily in terms of authority, decision making, and patterns of group behavior.

[13] See, for example, Herbert A. Simon, *Administrative Behavior: A Study of Decision-making Processes in Administrative Organization* (New York: The Macmillan Company, 1947).

[14] In addition to the volumes already cited, I would mention also Herbert A. Simon, Donald W. Smithburg, and Victor A. Thompson, *Public Administration* (New York: Alfred A. Knopf, Inc., 1950); Robert Tannenbaum, Irving R. Weschler, and Fred Massarik, *Leadership and Organization: A Behavioral Science Approach* (New York: McGraw-Hill Book Company, Inc., 1961); Victor A. Thompson, *Modern Organization* (New York: Alfred A. Knopf, Inc., 1961); and Chris Argyris, "The Individual and Organization: An Empirical Test," *Administrative Science Quarterly*, vol. 4 (September, 1959), p. 145.

2. No one system of cooperative effort can be said with scientific accuracy to be superior to another in terms of efficiency (utilization of resources). The basic criterion of organizational effectiveness is leadership which succeeds in developing a favorable response from external power groups and in promoting a continuing commitment to a high level of productive effort on the part of the internal staff.

3. Individuals who make up a system of cooperative effort respond to their organizational environment in terms of certain felt needs, which include the need for physical and economic security, the need for a sense of personal worth, the need for acceptance (love) as a person, and the need to realize meaning from their activity and experience.

4. Decision making in an organization seeks to evoke motivations and inducements on the part of individuals and groups to participate in a common enterprise: to accept the goals of the enterprise, to identify themselves with these goals, and to seek their achievement.

5. Organization as a pattern of status subordination for various individuals and groups may promote frustration which finds outlet in turnover, unionism, excessive ambition to rise in the hierarchy, criticism of and hostility toward superiors, a primary concern for monetary rewards, and apathy.

6. Conflict arises among individuals and groups within an organization when decisions threaten the satisfaction derived from participation in the work of the organization or when decisions suggest an uncertain future.

7. By the very fact of their existence, organizations as entities develop certain behavioral characteristics: they seek to perpetuate themselves, to preserve their internal harmony and well-being, and to achieve growth.

8. Conflict arises among organizational entities when the goals or activities of one appear to threaten the security or growth of another.

There is no need here to consider these propositions in detail. Nor do we need to assess the merits of the behavioral observations of organization in comparison with the more formalistic structural approach.

There are many other subjects besides those outlined above which the behavioral scholars discuss. For example, they lay stress upon informal as opposed to formal organization, that is, leadership based upon group acceptance rather than actual title and position. They are much concerned also with the process of communication.

It may be useful to note in passing, however, that some persons have apparently come to the conclusion that discussion of organization in either structural or behavioral terms does not advance our knowledge about organizational entities. Accordingly, it is suggested that attention be concentrated upon the "administrative process." Or it is proposed that decision making be the focus of attention. We would then accept the fact of organizational entities and seek to understand how they operate rather than how they are structured.

For example, the administrative process has been

described as consisting of five types of activities.[15] These are (1) decision making, (2) programming, (3) communicating, (4) controlling, and (5) reappraising. Furthermore, the administrative process has an "action cycle" which consists of (1) policy (the definition of objectives), (2) the allocation of resources (people, money, authority, and materials) for the accomplishment of defined objectives, and (3) execution (the integration and synthesis of effort). Finally, it is suggested that each action cycle has a preeminent value to realize and conserve. Policy seeks purposive direction of effort. The allocation of resources seeks economy—I would prefer to use the word "efficiency." And execution seeks "dynamic coordination."

It seems to me that such an outline of administrative process has certain utility for the study of an organizational entity but that it does not particularly advance our understanding of organizational problems or avoid their importance. This emphasis upon process places organizational issues in the larger context of purpose and operation. We are still left with structural and behavioral questions about how to assign specialization effectively and how to integrate endeavor into some general whole.

The discussion of decision making likewise has its utility and its limitations. For example, Talcott Parsons has identified three categories of decisions.[16] First, there are *policy decisions*. These are the decisions which commit an organization as a whole and

---

[15] Edward H. Litchfield, *op. cit.*, p. 3.
[16] Talcott Parsons, *op. cit.*, pp. 30–33.

determine its primary objectives. Decisions which affect the type of business product, the quality of product, the scale of operations, the attitude toward clientele, and the attitude toward employees fall in this category. Secondly, there are *allocative decisions.* Decisions which determine the resources of men, materials, facilities, equipment, and financing fall in this category. Thirdly, there are *coordination decisions,* which have to do with integration of the organizational parts of an enterprise.

In a recent series of lectures, Herbert Simon has suggested that decision making may be divided into three phases.[17] The first phase is *intelligence,* a survey of the economic, technical, political, and social environment of action. The second phase is *design,* the development or invention of various possible courses of action. The third phase is *choice,* the selection of a particular course of action from among alternatives. Simon divides the substance of all such decisions of choice into two further categories: *programmed* and *nonprogrammed.* Programmed decisions are repetitive and routine, involving the application of settled policy or instructions to particular circumstances. The pricing of articles for sale, the reordering of supplies for stockage in a warehouse, the determination of an employee's rights to sick leave—these are examples of programmed decisions. Nonprogrammed decisions, on the other hand, are novel and unstructured, involving issues which are new and important to the purpose and welfare of an organization. The question whether

[17] Herbert A. Simon, *The New Science of Management Decision* (New York: Harper & Brothers, 1960).

a business entity should buy out a competitor or manufacture a new product would be examples of nonprogrammed decisions. Simon then proposes that new techniques of operations research and problem solving may extend human capacity to deal effectively with programmed and nonprogrammed decisions.

These and other discussions of decision making notably advance our awareness of administrative operation. They still do not afford any real understanding of organization in either its structural or behavioral characteristics.

The Continuing Influence of Weber

I have already mentioned the name of Max Weber, the German sociologist whose writings on the subject of bureaucracy early in this century seem to have made a lasting impression upon American sociologists and others.[18] Weber identified two major characteristics of bureaucracy, by which he meant large-scale, organized endeavor. These two characteristics were authority and hierarchy. The two aspects of bureaucracy were closely related.

Authority seemed to mean several things to Weber. It meant a defined or fixed area of jurisdiction for an official. It meant the power to give commands. It meant the regular and continuous fulfillment of assigned duties. He went on to say that in "lawful" government these three elements constituted bureaucratic authority and that in private economic enter-

[18] See for example, Robert K. Merton, Ailsa P. Gray, Barbara Hockey, Hanan C. Selvin, eds., *Reader in Bureaucracy* (Glencoe, Ill.: Free Press, 1952).

prise they constituted "bureaucratic management." [19] Weber did not dwell at length upon "lawful" government or how such government might create or delegate authority. He observed bureaucracy in terms of the governmental administrative agency as such, or within the business enterprise.

Secondly, Weber propounded the idea that bureaucracy was characterized by hierarchy, by a clearly defined structure of graded authority. Hierarchy meant a firmly ordered system of superordination and subordination in the relationships of individuals one to the other. Weber could not conceive of an aggregation of persons working together except under the principle of hierarchy in which each "lower" office was under the control and supervision of a "higher" one.

Regardless of how much American scholars and practitioners may disagree about the particular pattern of organizational structure which should exist in a government agency or a business enterprise, they have accepted without further analysis the concepts of authority and hierarchy. The behavioral theorists almost without exception presuppose a hierarchy of administrative authority in an organization. They are unwilling to prescribe an organizational structure, but they begin immediately to describe human behavior within a particular scheme of hierarchical relationships. The behavioral theorists seem unable to postulate any other kind of organizational pattern.

In consequence, more or less without question American scholars and analysts of organization have

[19] Gerth and Mills, *op. cit.,* chap. VIII.

accepted the concept of hierarchy. Moreover, with the use of the word "bureaucracy" to mean any large enterprise or identifiable entity producing goods or services for public consumption, the idea of hierarchy has been automatically applied to every such endeavor.

Application to Higher Education

Consciously or unconsciously, much of the thinking about the organization and operation of colleges and universities in the United States has been affected by the kind of analysis of organizational structure which I have tried to sketch here. Few persons, especially trustees, administrators, and faculty members, realize the extent to which their own ideas have been influenced by the organizational concepts around which we have built so much of our knowledge about public and business administration.

For example, it is customary to describe a board of trustees as having ultimate or final authority for all activities of a college or university. When such a prescription is perceived as not quite corresponding to fact, and when a struggle for power seems imminent between faculty and trustees, it is customary to say that in their wisdom the trustees have seen fit to delegate a large measure of authority over strictly academic matters to the faculty. It is an act of great generosity, or of great self-denial, on the part of trustees which is ordinarily offered as explanation for faculty power. We cannot find any other way by which to square the concept of a hierarchical structuring of

authority with the reality of faculty determination of
academic policy.

After all, the confusion is understandable. Super-
ficially, there may appear to be a hierarchy of offices
in a college or university. It is often pictured as a suc-
cession of positions from instructor to assistant professor to associate professor to professor to department
chairman to dean to academic vice president to president to board of trustees. Does not such an arrangement meet the usual representation of hierarchy and
authority in organizations?

Moreover, in many other respects colleges and
universities appear on first glance to resemble the ordinary concepts of organizational structure. A college
or university is purposive, having more or less well-de-
fined objectives in instruction, research, and public
service to realize. There is specialization of effort in
the college or university. We recognize various disciplines and professional fields of study, together with
subspecializations in almost every field. There are also
numerous technical specializations needed for the operation of the college or university as an entity, from
admission of students, student record keeping, and
various student services to the purchase of supplies,
the recording of financial accounts, and the maintenance of buildings. We recognize also integration of
specializations by departments, colleges and schools,
institutes and centers, and various administrative offices. There is presumably a structure of educational
leadership beginning with the president and board
of trustees.

When we turn to the behavioral approach to

organization, again we encounter superficial similarities. The behavioral theorists recognize work specialization, integration, authority, and hierarchy. They emphasize the importance of leadership. They caution that organization means people working together, and that people must be motivated to accept goals and to seek their accomplishment. The behavioral theorist acknowledges the existence of conflict, as well as certain peculiar attachments to security, status, and organizational self-preservation. These and other matters of concern to the behavioral theorists can be identified in most if not all colleges and universities.

The question then immediately presents itself: Why should not a college or university as an acknowledged organizational entity be thought of as essentially similar to the organizations in governmental and business administration from which in general our ideas about organization have been developed? This is an important question. It deserves careful attention.

Let me state my own answer immediately and succinctly. I believe strongly that a college or university has little if any resemblance to the generalized conceptions of organization which may be applicable to certain types of governmental administrative agencies and certain types of business entities. To look to the ideas on organization summarized herein for guidance in the understanding of a college or university or for prescription of desirable structure is completely to misconceive the nature of the institution of higher education.

Scholars of public administration and of business

administration have been guilty of a major omission. In public administration, for example, there has been a tendency to begin study and analysis with a particular problem: civil service reform, budget and accounting improvement, or economy and efficiency as exemplified by centralized purchasing, integration of related administrative activities, and simplification of procedures. Organizational improvement has often been confused with a major development in American political institutions: the strengthening of the role of the executive in his relationship to the legislative and judicial branches of government.

The point is that in this concentration upon specific problem areas and certain ostensibly limited goals of administrative economy and efficiency, the scholar of public administration has largely ignored the broader context of his subject: the American political system. Public administration is a part of government. It cannot be separated from an understanding of American political reality: the political traditions of the United States, the structure of political power in society and how this power manifests itself, and the structure of political institutions.[20]

Ideas about organization of administrative activity have been formulated too largely in a vacuum, where scholars have endeavored to ignore political tradition, political power, and political institutions. The validity of many of these ideas is suspect for this

---

[20] As a political scientist, I have endeavored to describe the political institutions of our nation in relation to administrative activity in my *Government and Public Administration* (New York: McGraw-Hill Book Company, Inc., 1959).

very reason. Or, to express my criticism in a different way, scholars of public administration have been content to say that administrative organization is purposive without exploring that purpose in its rich background of history, the politics of power, and the American institution of government.

The same kind of criticism may be leveled at much of the discussion of business administration which has gone on in this country. Recently two careful studies have been made of the deficiencies in education for business administration in the United States.[21] Both emphasize the necessity of giving more attention to the subject of the "market environment." This means actually greater attention to the institution of the American economy. Presumably, this need is not to be met simply by a course in elementary economics, with its concern for consumption and demand, market price, and national income components. Rather, an understanding of the institution of economic enterprise made up of producers and consumers would become a major consideration in every important segment of study, including the analysis of organizational entities.

It is the basic purpose of an institution of society and how this purpose conditions both organization structure and operation of the individual units of the institution which is so frequently overlooked in or-

[21] Robert A. Gordon and James E. Howell, *Higher Education for Business* (New York: Columbia University Press, 1959); and Frank C. Pierson and others, *The Education of American Businessmen* (New York: McGraw-Hill Book Company, Inc., 1959).

ganizational study. It is the basic purpose of the institution of government which is largely ignored in most discussions of the organization of public administration. It is the basic purpose of the institution of the economy which is largely ignored in most discussions of the organization of business enterprise.

Furthermore, we have given only lip service to the idea that purpose conditions organization. We acknowledge that organization is purposive, but we tend to think of purpose as limited and specific—to protect public health or to manufacture an automobile—without relating it to broader concepts of the public welfare and good government or of free enterprise and maximum employment and production. We tend to forget that broad purposes may have some influence upon the more limited objectives and processes of a separate administrative or business entity.

I have suggested already that in our examination of administrative and business organization we often tend to forget the great variety of entities which serve the purposes of government and the economy. There is much more variety than we often acknowledge, from the government corporation and the regulatory commission to the school district and the mental health department. There is even greater variety among mining, manufacturing, farming, commercial, finance, banking, service, and other economic endeavors. There is some real doubt whether attempts to prescribe details of organizational arrangement for these varied enterprises have been more than intelligent guesses.

Certainly Weber's observation about authority and hierarchy was full of insight and was highly useful in terms of hypothesis. He was not a careful investigator prepared to demonstrate the validity of his ideas with a large array of empirical evidence. Furthermore, although Weber had visited the United States and traveled for reasons of health in many European countries, he made only fragmentary use of comparative data. He knew the Prussian and imperial civil service of pre-World War I days. He did not conceive of the plurality of social structure which has characterized the United States and has influenced the organization and operation of its institutions.

It is little wonder then that many who have examined the organization of American colleges and universities in the light of the usual concepts of work specialization, of integration by hierarchy and authority, and of leadership through management are dismayed and troubled.[22]

The internal organization of a college or university does not resemble that of the Army and Navy, or of the Department of Agriculture, or of the Atomic Energy Commission, or of the Federal Trade Commission, or of the Department of Highways in a state government, or of the Department of Sanitation in a large municipality. The internal organization of a college or university does not resemble that of a steel

[22] One perceives the sense of amazement if not of outright disapproval even in so sympathetic a volume as that by John J. Corson, *Governance of Colleges and Universities* (New York: McGraw-Hill Book Company, Inc., 1960).

company, a department store, a bank, or a hotel. Colleges and universities are different. They are different in institutional setting, in purpose, in operation, and hence in internal organization.

It is the difference which we shall explore in subsequent chapters.

Chapter 2

Higher Education
As an Institution

HIGHER EDUCATION is a unique institution in Western society generally and in the United States in particular. It is customary to speak of higher education as having three primary purposes: instruction, research, and public service. Actually, the public service referred to is vitally related to instruction and research, involving dissemination of knowledge on a continuing basis or the performance of activities essential to instruction. It might more appropriately be said that higher education seeks to preserve, transmit, and advance knowledge.

This is a peculiar purpose—peculiar in that it is served only by higher education. It might be mentioned that institutions of society—the family, the economy, the church, the government, and others—tend to be differentiated one from another not just in structure but more importantly in function. No two serve the same purpose. The identifying characteristic of a social institution is its particular objective which marks it off from any other institution. So it is with higher education. It serves a peculiar purpose, and hence is a unique or identifiable institution.

Knowledge is a precious and illusive thing. Bacon long ago described knowledge itself as power. So it is: the power to guide action, to make one person and one group and one nation superior to others, to influence the life and well-being of others. Knowledge of how to produce and distribute goods, how to guide and direct others, how to protect and advance the public weal, how to undertake the pursuit of personal satisfaction—such knowledge is much in demand today as in ages past. But knowledge is not easy to identify or to discover. Knowledge seldom seems complete; it always seems to present new challenges.

Higher education has made its province the realm of knowledge. This knowledge may be inherently valuable for its own sake, for the satisfaction it brings to the individual who seeks to escape ignorance and superstition. This knowledge may be useful in solving human problems from health to production, from justice to unemployment. Knowledge for its own sake and for use—knowledge is what higher education would impart.

As an institution with this special purpose—to preserve, transmit, and advance knowledge—higher education has over the years evolved in an amazing way. It has seemed at times to be a part of other social institutions or to take on their peculiar characteristics of operation. Higher education has at times appeared to be a religious institution. At times it has appeared to be a part of the market place where goods and services are produced and distributed. At other times it is an eleemosynary institution, a part of a system of voluntary support by which society seeks to meet its obligations to help others with a generous and benevolent hand. And yet higher education is none of these institutions in fact. It has been closely allied with other institutions in history. It behaves in patterns reminiscent of other institutions. Through all these similarities, it remains apart, peculiar, different, custodian through the ages of the higher learning.

Higher Education as a Religious Institution

In its origins in the medieval world, higher education was clerical, and some of the medieval customs and costumes survive to this day as a reminder of religious beginnings. The university of the Middle Ages, from which in direct descent our colleges and universities of today have evolved, was an outgrowth of cathedral schools and monasteries.[1] As universities emerged early in the twelfth century, they were something more than an ecclesiastical agency. The student body and the masters (the teachers and scholars) were regarded as clerks, as part of the great body of churchmen of the time. Yet these persons were not necessarily members of religious orders. And while the university

[1] Scholars will, of course, know Hastings Rashdall, *The Universities of Europe in the Middle Ages,* edited by F. M. Powicke and A. B. Emden (New York: Oxford University Press, 1936). This is the second edition of the great three-volume work originally published in 1895.

functioned under the general oversight of ecclesiastical authority, conflict between the two was not unknown.

To a considerable degree, society in Western Europe in the Middle Ages was either feudal or clerical. At the base of feudal society was the serf or peasant, for all practical purposes tied to his land. At the apex of this hierarchy was the Roman Emperor, at least in theory, and in practice a king or other ruler of a large area. The medieval town with its merchant and craft guilds impaired the symmetry of this social system. The clerical world, on the other hand, centering in a supposedly universal church, was at least a structure based upon individual ability, thanks to the rule of celibacy. It was quite natural that in such a bifurcated society the university should find itself primarily allied with the church.

The educated clerk became a teacher, an ecclesiastical official, the member of a religious order, or in time a civil servant. A considerable career was open to his ambition and effort, but this was true primarily because of his clerical status. If high officials of the church became even more nationalistic than the kings they served, their rise to positions of political power was made possible in large degree because of their clerical—that is, their educated—background.

With all its disruption of the political, social, and economic fabric of the sixteenth century, the Reformation brought likewise its changes in the position of the university. Luther was highly critical of universities as he knew them, but Protestant states found it convenient to continue them under their own direction. The international characteristic of many universities, such as the one at Paris, suffered under the division of Europe into two warring religious camps. And a new orthodoxy was expected of the universities. Yet fundamentally the university was still thought of as an appendage of the church, or closely allied to it, even when the church as in England and certain German states was no longer Roman Catholic.

The college as it was transplanted to colonial America from England in the seventeenth century still had a decidedly religious bias. Harvard was established in 1636 in large part, according to the well-known statement of Puritan principles, "to advance learning and perpetuate it to posterity; dreading to leave an illiterate ministry to the churches, when our present ministers shall lie in the dust." Other colleges were founded in the eighteenth century for similar purposes. Yet these colleges in the New World were more than religious seminaries, even as were the universities of Western Europe. Moreover, Protestant society, in the process of struggling toward religious toleration and freedom, was providing a widening role for higher education. Still in the first decades of the nineteenth century in the United States most American colleges, as Professor Hofstadter has pointed out, "were not only religious, in the broad sense, but actually under denominational control and under the leadership of clerical presidents." [2]

[2] Richard Hofstadter, "The Development of Higher Education in America," in Hofstadter and C. DeWitt Hardy, *The Development and Scope of Higher Education in the United States* (New York: Columbia University Press, 1952), p. 9.

The period after the Civil War in the United States witnessed a great transformation from the age of the college to the age of the university.[3] It was a process accompanied by a growing secularization of higher education. The higher learning and religious faith knew at best an uneasy truce; at worst, they engaged in bitter and fruitless warfare. In 100 years the ties of higher education and religion in the United States have largely been severed. Yet the relationship has by no means been completely ended. The two institutions continue to share common concerns and to seek a basic unity in which knowledge and faith realize complementary rather than competing contributions to man's life.

The role of the church in higher education in the United States is by no means negligible. A recent listing of some 2,000 colleges and universities by the Office of Education indicates that nearly 800 of these remain "related" to a religious denomination, of which nearly 500 are related to Protestant denominations and nearly 300 to the Roman Catholic Church. To be sure, close to 80 of these are entirely devoted to education in theology. Yet nine-tenths of the total number are engaged in liberal and professional programs of higher education.

"Related to a religious denomination" is a difficult term to define. In the instance of most colleges and universities related to Protestant denominations, other than theological seminaries, "related to" means that some church body officially elects all or a substan-

---

[3] The designations are those employed by Professor Hofstadter, *ibid.*

tial part of the trustees. In addition, in varying amounts the parent church body, usually on an area or regional basis, may contribute some direct financial support to the operation of these colleges and universities. In the instance of Roman Catholic colleges, "related to" means usually that a religious order of the Catholic Church has established and operates a college or university in a particular community. Ordinarily such colleges and universities receive no direct financial support from and have few if any formal ties to the diocese of the area. On the other hand, a goodly part of the support of such colleges and universities comes from the contributed services of teaching members of the order, and necessarily the order retains substantial authority of direction over the work of the college or university.

Even so, it is possible in many instances involving Protestant, Jewish, and Roman Catholic colleges and universities to exaggerate the degree of external church control. Such church authority as exists is apt to be exercised with considerable moderation. Thus, trustees elected by a Protestant conference or synod may in effect be self-perpetuating. And a religious order of the Roman Catholic Church may leave extensive discretion in academic matters to the administrative officers and faculty of the individual college or university.

Furthermore, many so-called "nondenominational" colleges and universities may operate a school of theology and otherwise maintain close working relationships with one or more religious denominations. And it is not uncommon for public colleges and universities to have a department of religion or of religious education and to provide informal discussions of religous subjects.

The institution of higher education as it is known in the United States has not entirely escaped from its clerical origins. Nor is there reason to believe that it necessarily should. Even as in the medieval university, a concern with theology and the philosophy, art, and literature of religion remains a continuing and important cultural preoccupation of higher education.

Yet in spite of this long association, our colleges and universities in the twentieth century do not belong to any church in any real sense. Colleges and universities belong to the world of knowledge. A church-related college opens its doors to students of all religious denominations; no religious test is applied for admission. While some formal study in religion may be required of the student who is a communicant of the church to which the college or university is related, this requirement is not usually applied to other students. The objective of a college or university is not to be religious but to be intellectual in a rigorous, determined way. No college or university can survive upon faith. It must conserve, transmit, and advance knowledge.

Higher Education as a Welfare Institution

The university of the Middle Ages and of later times was an object of charity. Kings and princes, noblemen and merchants provided endowments which built great buildings and which provided operating income. Because of its religious connection, the university was an appropriate recipient of benevolence. It was blessed to give to the medieval university, just as today it is comforting to contribute to our colleges and universities.

The college and university became an eleemosynary agency for a simple reason. If young men who came from the lower gentry and the yeoman class of society were to be educated, their education had to be subsidized. It is interesting to realize that nearly one thousand years ago higher education was not thought of as the privilege of nobility and wealth but as the province of persons of talent, wherever in society these might be found. Undoubtedly, the children of serfs were ignored, as well as the progeny of the medieval slums. But youth of lesser social status and younger sons of nobility might be destined for clerical careers, and once within the confines of the university it was talent which rose to the top.

Such a system of education open to youth of varied status was possible only through the subsidy of the university. Great churchmen joined great lords in contributing to the support of universities. The practice was so widespread as to become part of an accepted way of finance, continuing until this very day.

As we have noted, social mobility was at one time possible only within the clerical order. There were occasional exceptions through military prowess. As cities prospered and brought new classes into existence, more opportunity for individual achievement occurred. Higher education remained an avenue of advancement. This was noticeable in the English university of Protestant times, in the seventeenth and eighteenth centuries, as well as in the universities in Catholic nations of the same period.

The American college inherited the welfare tradition. In the Colonies, colleges were early established to provide opportunity for youth of varied social backgrounds to qualify for religious, legal, and other professions. One colonial college was even intended as a missionary enterprise to the Indians. In the early Republic, colleges under private and state sponsorship dotted the frontier, promoting educational opportunity in a society which gave special importance to self-confidence, equality, and local autonomy. In such an atmosphere the means of education were to be forever encouraged.

In order for youth of ability to have equal access to higher education, regardless of economic or social status, some special provision had to be made to find ways in which young people might attend college at small personal cost. One method was to raise funds through gifts with which to build facilities and with which to defray current operating costs. In this way higher education took on the special characteristics of a welfare institution.

Since the time of its medieval origins, the institution of higher education has always been economically poor. Its object has not been to make money but to lose money. Our colleges and universities have remained in the category of a charitable undertaking. This fact is indicated by several situations. One is the philanthropic nature of much of the financial support of higher education. Another characteristic is the tax-exempt status enjoyed by colleges and universities. Still another factor is the customary description of higher education as a "nonprofit" enterprise.

Today philanthropy is practiced on a sizable scale in the United States. It is estimated that as much as 8 billion dollars is contributed annually by various individuals, corporations, and private foundations to charitable and educational purposes.[4] Of this total, approximately 16 per cent goes to education: schools, colleges, and universities.

The welfare nature of higher education is peculiarly important in the United States because of the substantial number of students enrolled in colleges and universities functioning under private sponsorship. If we except the junior colleges, we find today that about 45 per cent of all students attend privately sponsored colleges and universities. The publicly sponsored colleges and universities—mostly operating under state financing—would be seriously pressed to accept a substantially larger proportion of students. Furthermore, the existence of colleges and universities under private sponsorship may set standards of excellence and freedom which are useful indeed for the publicly sponsored colleges and universities. For these and other reasons, there is considerable effort expended in the United States to preserve and strengthen the status of that segment of higher education functioning under private sponsorship.

[4] *Giving U.S.A.,* 1961 edition (New York: American Association of Fund-Raising Counsel, Inc.).

The continuance of privately sponsored colleges and universities depends in large measure upon adequate gift support. In this sense the welfare characteristic of higher education remains important.

Even in the instance of state-sponsored colleges and universities, private gift support on a welfare basis has its usefulness. Many buildings have been provided by voluntary giving. The maintenance of student aid programs, the encouragement of certain kinds of research, and the enrichment of instructional programs may depend in considerable degree upon gifts from individuals and private foundations. The publicly sponsored college or university in the United States is by no means 100 per cent publicly financed. In many instances state tax funds may provide no more than one-third of total current operating expenditures. The remaining income may be derived from student charges, federal government research and other grants, various charges, and philanthropy.

Both privately and publicly sponsored colleges and universities are eager to expand their gift income. They thus acknowledge their kinship to a voluntary welfare institution.

Higher Education as an Economic Institution

In one sense every institution of society is economic; it must have some method of earning income if it is to survive in a system of specialized production. In our society we know only three principal methods of economic survival. One method is for a person or group of persons to sell a product or service to other individuals or groups. This is the prevailing concept of the market place in the economy of the American people. The individual obtains his personal income by the sale of his services on this same market. A second method is to obtain economic support through a tax upon the market or upon individuals in a society. This is the way in which government operates. A third method is for an indivdual or group to receive gifts on a voluntary basis from other persons.

To the extent that higher education receives gifts for its financial support it is a welfare institution. To the extent that higher education receives tax support it is an agency of government. To the extent that higher education sells a product or a service it is part of the economic institution in our society which operates through the market place.[5]

In recent years there have been several studies of the "economics" of higher education in terms of various sources of income and various objects of expenditure.[6] Only certain selected items of this economic analysis need be mentioned here. Higher education

[5] Obviously, I have ignored the process whereby income for current expenditure or capital formation is obtained by borrowing from others. I have also omitted the practice whereby government may obtain income by the simple though usually dangerous process of making (printing) money for its own use.

[6] Among many articles and books on this subject, I would refer here particularly to Dexter M. Keezer, ed., *Financing Higher Education, 1960–70* (New York: McGraw-Hill Book Company, Inc., 1959); and Seymour E. Harris, ed., *Higher Education in the United States: The Economic Problems* (Cambridge, Mass.: Harvard University Press, 1960).

as an institution is concerned about the resources required to provide the quantity and quality of educational service needed by the American society. These needs are determined in accordance with cultural tradition and current social policy. A society requires a certain quality and quantity of education in order to provide a given proportion of youth with higher education in varying degrees of specialization and depth. In the light of these educational objectives, the needs for economic resources are calculated. The needs come first. How to obtain the resources to meet these needs is a second consideration.

A different kind of economic analysis has been undertaken by Prof. Theodore W. Schultz.[7] It is concerned with the impact of education in general and higher education in particular upon the total economic activity of American society. Professor Schultz looks upon education as a human investment. He holds that there are fruits of education which consist of improvements in the capacity of people to produce economic wealth. The health of a working population, the technological skill of a working force, the availability of finance capital—all these factors play a large part in determining the economic output or gross national product of a society. Moreover, all these factors are enhanced by education in general and

[7] Theodore W. Schultz, "Education and Economic Growth," in *Social Forces Influencing American Education—1961,* Sixtieth Yearbook of the National Society for the Study of Education (Chicago: University of Chicago Press, 1961), p. 46.

higher education in particular. To the degree that higher education contributes through knowledge to increased economic output it has advanced the economic growth of a society. Professor Schultz argues that education is an investment in human capital just as a factory is an investment in physical plant capital.

Professor Schultz estimates that in 1956 nearly 29 billion dollars was expended in all forms of educational endeavor, of which about one-third represented the economic resources employed by higher education. This outlay included an allowance for income which students forego by being enrolled in education rather than in the labor force. At the same time, Professor Schultz estimates that the investment return to the individual upon the cost of his higher education as a result of increased earnings above those of a high school education may be around 9 per cent. He also argues that a goodly portion of increased economic output in our society must be attributed to this investment in human capital; it cannot all be attributed to investment in physical plant.

Professor Schultz does not suggest that the investment return of higher education necessarily implies a particularly desirable method of financing. It may still be desirable to obtain income in the three principal ways known to our society. On the other hand, Prof. Seymour E. Harris insists, primarily upon the grounds of expediency, that an increasingly larger share of the total resources needed by higher education must be charged to the individual student. In effect, this is an argument that higher education should become more of an economic institution, pricing its product (educational service) at a level to meet costs (needed resources).

Professor Harris points out that about 25 per cent of the educational and general income of higher education was obtained from charges to students in 1958, and he estimates that about 40 per cent of such income will be provided from student charges by 1970.[8] As of 1960 the total current operating expenditures of higher education were probably 5.5 to 6 billion dollars. It seems likely that nearly 40 per cent of this total amount was derived from student charges, since almost all auxiliary service income results from charges to students.

If we were to consider certain research activities as being in the nature of services rendered for a charge to the federal government, we would probably find that well over 50 per cent of all income for higher education at the present time resembles "earned" income. Although the motivation of a desire for profit is lacking in higher education, it seems fairly obvious that in substantial degree higher education as an institution is taking on characteristics of the market economy. There may be a trend indeed in this direction, not from desire or intent but from necessity.

It must be remembered that the figures cited here pertain to higher education as a whole and do not differentiate between state, local, and federal government sponsored colleges and universities on the one hand and privately sponsored colleges and universities

[8] See his "Financing of Higher Education: Broad Issues," in Keezer, *op. cit.*, p. 36.

on the other hand. It is probable that the trend toward behavior as an enterprise allied to a market economy is even more pronounced among the privately sponsored colleges and universities than among the publicly sponsored colleges and universities.

Higher Education as a Part of Government

The state became interested in higher education almost as early as the church. There are documents indicating imperial concern with universities and their students in the twelfth century, not too long after the universities began to emerge from their cathedral school and monastic origins. In the next three centuries there were several instances of imperial and kingly charters to new universities. And many of the universities founded under church auspices soon enjoyed noble patronage.

It was natural for the state to concern itself with higher education. At best there was ever an uneasy truce between spiritual and temporal power in medieval society. The state could not afford to permit the education of its clerks to fall entirely into church hands and hope to maintain the substance of its claim to jurisdiction over the immediate life of man. In order to obtain some balance of power in the earthly struggle of churchmen and statesmen, the state had to extend its interest to higher education. It is an interest which has never waned.

The governmental interests of our nation in the realm of higher education today are largely twofold. Government has an interest in the education of our citizenry. A democratic society presupposes wide-scale educational attainment among the people. A democratic society furthermore seeks to promote an elite of talent rather than an aristocracy of status and wealth. Our government is concerned to promote social mobility, and no means to this end is of more importance than education, including higher education. Government is also concerned to promote economic well-being, and education is an important means here as well. Secondly, and more recently, higher education is a stake in the cold war. In the struggle for world domination between Russia and the United States, higher education has a vital part in enlarging the resources of strength. To be indifferent to higher education is to be indifferent to our national security.

There is no need here to trace the history of governmental concern with higher education in the United States. It was evident in colonial days in the support given to supposedly "private" colleges. It was evident in the Northwest Ordinance of 1787. The new states joining the Union after 1789 were encouraged to create seminaries of learning and were given land grants to help finance their operations. In 1862 the federal government provided further land-grant assistance to colleges or universities set up in the various states to give instruction, among other subjects, in agriculture and the mechanic arts. But the principal support for higher education has come from state governments themselves, primarily through state-sponsored universities. Local governments have established universities in only a few instances, although some 250 junior colleges operate through local school districts or other special arrangements. The federal government has confined its direct chartering of universities under federal sponsorship to military academies, Howard University, and one or two others.

Government has assisted the privately sponsored colleges and universities by exempting their property used for educational purposes from the general property tax, on occasion by exempting them from state sales taxes, and by exempting gifts from federal and state income taxes. In a few instances, state governments have directly or indirectly channeled tax funds to privately sponsored colleges and universities.

Both government support and government encouragement of higher education have expressed a public interest in providing educational opportunity for youth. To have a portion of our citizenry educated in colleges and universities has become increasingly important over the years. This fact is clearly evident in the ever larger percentage of youth enrolling in our colleges and universities from 1900 to 1960.

In the past twenty years, however, a new dimension has been added to government interest in higher education. This concern began with World War II when above all else the federal government looked to American universities for assistance in research and development activities. The atomic bomb was only the most spectacular achievement of this partnership; it was by no means the only important accomplishment. After the war, federal government research support to American universities continued, and in the past decade this support has steadily expanded until today it reaches almost 1 billion dollars a year. More-over, the research assistance is made directly to uni-versities regardless of whether they are publicly or privately sponsored.

In 1950 the federal government's housing laws were amended to make colleges and universities, public and private, eligible to borrow funds for dor-mitories and related facilities. After a change in the interest rate formula in 1955, considerable use began to be made of this program. More recently, through the National Defense Act of 1958 a whole new array of activities of public and private colleges and uni-versities became recipients of federal government financial assistance.

These and other governmental actions, both current and proposed, have developed primarily be-cause of the importance of higher education to the national security of the United States. Nor does this importance seem likely to diminish in the years ahead. On the contrary, governmental financial assistance to colleges and universities to educate needed talents and to perform vital research will unquestionably grow.

In state governments, the cost of this assistance has necessarily increased as state universities have expanded in enrollment, in the quality and level of educational programs undertaken, and in public serv-ice. With this enlarged cost has come a greater concern with the administrative operation of universities. Le-gal activities, the appointment of personnel, budget and other financial practices, the procurement of supplies, and the construction of buildings have come more and more under the supervision and control of various state agencies, such as the attorney general, the civil service commission, the state auditor, the state purchasing office, the state public works department, and the state budget office. Presumably all this supervision has been desirable in order to improve the efficiency of operation at state universities.

This tendency to make the state university simply another administrative agency of government had gone so far that during the 1950s many state university presidents and boards of trustees began to protest. One result of this effort was the publication in 1959 of a study and a declaration by a group of prominent citizens interested in state universities demanding a greater concern for the autonomy of the state university.[9]

For the institution of higher education as a whole in the United States, about 50 per cent of educational income and about 35 per cent of all current operating income are being provided by government. In terms of social purpose, our national security, and financial support, higher education has begun to assume more and more the appearance of an agency of government.

[9] Committee on Government and Higher Education, *The Efficiency of Freedom* (Baltimore: Johns Hopkins Press, 1959); and Malcolm Moos and Francis E. Rourke, *The Campus and the State* (Baltimore: Johns Hopkins Press, 1959). Dr. Milton S. Eisenhower, president of the Johns Hopkins University, served as chairman of the Committee.

Higher Education as a Unique Institution

It is readily evident that higher education possesses attributes of religion, private welfare, economic enterprise, and government administration. In terms of both tradition and current operating practice, higher education resembles other institutions and agencies of society. Yet higher education is not to be equated with any of these. Rather, our colleges and universities constitute a unique institution different from any other.

The peculiar institutional characteristics of higher education derive from the peculiar objective which the institution exists to serve: to preserve, transmit, and advance knowledge. The pursuit of this objective gives to higher education its partial resemblance to religion, welfare, the economy, and government. There are religious, welfare, economic, and governmental interests in the performance of our colleges and universities. Higher education is still unusual.

What gives higher education its unique status is its relation to society at large. The objective of higher education—the preservation, transmission, and advancement of knowledge—implies not just a belief in the importance of knowledge. There is, as well, a more practical goal: to enable individuals to develop their talents for the service of others. The use of knowledge by young persons of educated ability may ever be a threat to those who already hold and exercise power in society.

Education is a dangerous business. It is committed to change. It expects first of all to change individuals by augmenting their store of knowledge and by developing their ability to reason. Beyond this, the educated person may become an instrument of social change. By the discovery and utilization of knowledge in biology and medicine, we may conquer disease; by the discovery and utilization of knowledge in the physical sciences and engineering, we may create great new stores of material wealth, as well as great new instruments of military destruction. Higher education may be used in infinite ways to seek improvement in the social, economic, political, and voluntary patterns of human behavior. Creative change is the province of a higher education which is a part of society rather than an escape from it.

Higher education by its activity appears to threaten the positions of leadership in the established institutions of society. Higher education may question the ways and means by which men produce goods and services, the ways and means by which men live together, the ways and means by which men govern themselves and others, the ways and means by which men express their ultimate concern for the Ultimate. Higher education may declare that what is thought to be knowledge is no more than folklore and convention. Higher education is indispensable to any concept of material, biological, and spiritual progress, and at the same time it is a threat to the present power structure of society.

In many countries for many centuries, universities have been centers of social disturbance. In more recent years the issues have ranged from theories such as that of Darwin concerning natural selection which seems to refute the literal explanation of man's creation given in the Bible to theories such as that of Keynes concerning the equilibrium of a market economy in modern capitalism which seems to refute the idea of a "natural law" of economic behavior.

The essence of the objective to preserve, transmit, and advance knowledge is ever to question and ever to challenge the accepted ways of society. A democratic society devoted to the dignity of the individual and to the welfare of all should and does find this questioning tolerable. Even so, the institutions of economic, political, and social power in a democratic society may succumb on occasion to the practice of intolerance or even of tyranny. In an authoritarian society the status of higher education is precarious indeed. This fact is surely evident in the deplorable state of the study of the social sciences and the humanities in Russia.

The whole concern in the United States and in the Western world with academic freedom is an effort to acknowledge the unique relationship between higher education and society. Higher education is dangerous. It carries with it at all times the possibility that it may upset an existing power structure in society. It carries with it at all times the possibility that individuals and institutions in society may have to accept new ideas and new ways of behavior. The truth which higher education perpetuates and expands is never final but only tentative. At least this is the faith of scholars today.

A concept and practice of academic freedom have been necessary in Western society in order to provide maximum opportunity for the university to fulfill its mission in society.[10] Without a concept and practice of academic freedom, the institution of higher education cannot function fully or effectively. At the same time it seems clear that only in a free society can academic freedom hope to flourish with any vigor or reality.

In the United States it is sometimes said that the problem of academic freedom became real only with the emergence of the university after the Civil War. Prior to that time the American college had a relatively narrow and static curriculum. Then with the birth of the university in which graduate study and research became major preoccupations, there was an explosion of knowledge. The expansion which has taken place in the past 100 years is great indeed, and now we are concerned to increase the rate of advancement through enlarged expenditures for research. In any event, when knowledge is considered dynamic, and when the rate of growth in knowledge is to be speeded in the national interest, then academic freedom is essential.

The freedom which higher education seeks is noninterference from government and from various

[10] See Russell Kirk, *Academic Freedom* (Chicago: Henry Regnery Company, 1955); Robert M. MacIver, *Academic Freedom in Our Time* (New York: Columbia University Press, 1955); and Richard Hofstadter and Walter P. Metzger, *The Development of Academic Freedom in the United States* (New York: Columbia University Press, 1955).

groups in society in the exploration of new knowledge and in the discussion of the present state of knowledge in each field of academic interest. Colleges and universities do not seek to propagate knowledge outside their own walls, but the use made of knowledge occurs largely outside the institution of higher education itself.

In our society no wall separates the university from the world of everyday affairs. This is desirable, since the problems of current concern give additional meaning to the pursuit of knowledge, and knowledge illuminates the amelioration of problems. The student who is persuaded of new intellectual truth may as a practitioner of his profession seek to apply what he has learned. Business leaders interested in economic and technological growth may find it profitable to make use of new ideas generated in the university world. Political leaders may seek advice and assistance from scholars. In such ways as these, knowledge is carried into human affairs. Higher education as an institution generates knowledge. Individuals and other institutions must decide how to use it.

Higher Education and Organization

The peculiar institutional character and tradition of higher education are reflected in its organization. The purpose of such organization is to provide effective means for preserving, transmitting, and advancing knowledge. This purpose in turn requires a process whereby a certain degree of insulation may be realized between colleges and universities on the one hand and government and society on the other.

I purposefully speak of government and society as distinct. It is one of the basic propositions of a democratic society and polity that there is a difference between society and government. In a totalitarian society, government is everything; family, church, economy, voluntary association must serve the ends of the state and have no goals not approved by the state. In a democratic society, government is one of several social institutions, important but not dominant. In the United States we have not only a pluralism of social institutions but a pluralism of groups and of agencies within each institution.

In the realm of higher education in the United States there is no such thing as a system of colleges and universities in any cohesive, unified sense. We have no ministry of higher education in the federal government, and do not desire one. There has been some effort to create in effect ministries of higher education in the fifty states, although this attempt has been resisted by state-sponsored colleges and universities. At least the result of this effort would be fifty ministries, not one. Furthermore, of approximately 1,200 degree-granting colleges, professional schools, and universities in our country, some 800 operate as privately rather than publicly sponsored agencies.

Thus the institution of higher education in the United States has no central organizational structure but a wide variety of individual operating units. Such interrelationship as does exist is voluntary and usually extends to cooperation in limited areas of common concern without impairing the fundamental self-responsibility of each college and university.

A good deal of attention might be given to the subject of interrelationship between a college or university and society. A college or university cannot isolate itself from the society of which it is a part. As an institution, higher education is responsive to the influences of religion, philanthropy, the economy, and government. Drawing financial support from these various elements of society, higher education cannot very well ignore them. The world is very much with those who labor in the cause of higher education.

In this discussion I am much more concerned to dwell upon the internal organization of an individual college or university. There are two reasons for this. First, I believe there is more general misunderstanding about the subject of internal organization than about almost any other aspect of the American college or university. Moreover, this misunderstanding is just as widespread inside our colleges and universities as outside. Secondly, the attempt to insulate the college and university from the social passions of the moment has found its principal method one of internal organization.

For reasons already outlined, higher education has desired to avoid the manifestations of strong social authority from other institutions. In America absolute authority is as abhorrent in higher education as it is in the church, the economy, and the government. A pluralism of units of higher education, as I have just commented, is one of the fundamental procedures for avoiding such absolute authority.

At the same time, in terms of their own internal organization our colleges and universities have sought arrangements which would equally reflect this concern to avoid absolute authority. In this endeavor the colleges and universities have built up a practice of community as the fundamental basis of organization. This essay seeks to explain this practice of community.

Within the agencies of other institutions, such as particular religious denominations, particular business enterprises, and particular administrative agencies of government, the principle of a hierarchy of authority centering in a council or an administrator may be satisfactory. Within the agencies of higher education the principle of hierarchy with authority centering in a board or a single administrator is not satisfactory. It is not satisfactory in terms of the objective of higher education to preserve, transmit, and advance knowledge while enjoying a degree of insulation from social pressure outside the institution of higher education itself.

The principle of hierarchy applied to the internal organization of a college or university would permit an absolute authority to gain control of the individual unit. If the board were to exercise absolute authority over the operations of a college or university, then control of the board would achieve control of the college or university. Such control may be desirable in certain types of operations. For example, we cannot have political responsibility for governmental bureaucracy without control of the permanent officials by the instruments of government: legislative, executive, and judiciary. We cannot have maximum efficiency in industrial production without control of the activities of each component group contributing to the productive output. Such considerations as these are not operative in the instance of a college or university. The institutional and social role of colleges and universities is different, and the method of operation is different.

Instead of being organized upon the principle of a hierarchy of authority, our colleges and universities are organized internally upon the principle of a community of authority. Power is shared by four different constituent groups in the academic entity. These groups are faculty, students, alumni, and administration. Each group possesses substantial power. Such power might be used for self-destruction. In practice, the power of each constituent group is brought together in a community of authority which enables each college and university to pursue its noble purpose.

The goal of the academic community is to provide an *environment* of learning, not a *product* of learning. Knowledge is acquired by individuals. It is not an object to be built and used like an automobile, a piece of furniture, a house, or a pencil. To be sure, knowledge is divided into many fields with a great deal of specialization. There are specializations in techniques of study and research, such as aesthetics, historical and archaeological inquiry, the collection of empirical data, statistical and mathematical computation, laboratory experimentation, logical deduction and inference, the formulation of hypotheses, and conceptualization.

The scholar and the student have distinct but interrelated roles. The one preserves and transmits knowledge; the other absorbs. But there is the stimulus of interaction in the process of learning, and this may occur also in the conduct of research. The scholar has a high degree of commitment to the cause of education. The student is apt to be more concerned about the practical uses of knowledge.

The scholar and student labor as individuals. The goal of education is realized in individuals. It is conceivable that the learning process could be carried on with just one scholar and one student. Or one scholar could pursue his efforts alone, as might a single student. The college and university provide the convenience and even the necessity of scholarly association; they provide economies of common endeavor.

One final observation may be important. When we study the institution of government, we quickly perceive that in our country there is a sharing of power between central and state governments and a sharing of power between legislative, executive, and judicial branches. This is not a hierarchy of power but a sharing. If there is any hierarchy of power, it is within administrative agencies functioning under the supervision and control of these three branches of government.

The institution of government in America has avoided a hierarchy of power. Why then should we assume that other institutions would seek such a hierarchy? Within the institution of higher education, hierarchy of power has been avoided by a pluralism of agencies. But the avoidance of a concentration of power goes even further than this. Within each agency—that is, each college and university—there is an attempt in practice to avoid a hierarchy of power.

Community of power rather than a hierarchy of power is the organizational basis of American colleges and universities.

Chapter 3

Faculty

THE KEY ELEMENT in the academic process and in the academic community is the faculty. There is no other justification for the existence of a college or a university except to enable the faculty to carry on its instructional and research activities. Without a faculty higher education has no reason for being. It is the faculty which realizes or fails to realize the basic objectives of each college or university.

Yet there is no constituent group of the academic community which excites more continuing public concern than the faculty. The public press may from time to time give a good deal of attention to the antics of students, and on occasion alumni may present points of view which require attention. Students come and go. Alumni have other interests besides the operation of their alma mater. The faculty remains collectively at least as the center of academic interest.

Moreover, the organizational role of the faculty is often difficult to define with any precision. On the

65

one hand faculty members are often convinced that the operation of a college or university might well reside exclusively in their hands, although the exact machinery by which this would be done is seldom elaborated. On the other hand critics frequently assert that faculty members are impractical theorists: "No one of them has ever met a payroll" is the usual statement of derision. Neither extreme of faculty insistence upon academic power nor that of intemperate suspicion advances the organizational understanding of a college or university.

The Academic Profession

Before we examine in some detail the role of the faculty in the academic process and in academic decision making, we must first sketch certain aspects of the academic profession as it has developed in the United States. Unfortunately, we do not have many studies of the academic profession as such.[1] It would be helpful to have an analysis of the academic profession as comprehensive as the one which has recently been undertaken for the military profession.[2] Studies made in recent years tend to be concerned with particular aspects of the professor, such as his instructional

[1] Perhaps the best general description remains that provided by Logan Wilson, *The Academic Man* (New York: Oxford University Press, 1942).

[2] Morris Janowitz, *The Professional Soldier* (Glencoe, Ill.: Free Press, 1960).

tasks,[3] his economic status,[4] and his concern with academic freedom.[5]

The motivation of an individual to become a faculty member is probably compounded of many different influences. As an undergraduate student an individual may come under the spell of a dynamic and sympathetic teacher who encourages him to think of an academic career. Some members of the profession may be attracted by the prospect of independent endeavor. A few may follow in a parent's footsteps. Some may be interested in the prestige and status of the profession. Some may see in it an avenue to other more "exciting" opportunities.

At least it is possible to say that no one should enter the academic life unless he is devoted to the world of ideas and has a great desire to preserve, transmit, and advance knowledge. The academic profession demands of all its entrants that they be enamored of learning and have a deep-seated faith in the power of reason.

We know little about the social and economic status of those who decide to enter the profession. It seems probable that a great majority have come from the middle class of our society, and perhaps from the lower middle class as this is defined by the sociolo-

[3] John S. Diekhoff, *The Domain of the Faculty in Our Expanding Colleges* (New York: Harper & Brothers, 1956).
[4] Theodore Caplow and Reece J. McGee, *The Academic Market Place* (New York: Basic Books, Inc., 1958).
[5] Paul F. Lazarsfeld and Wagner Thielens, Jr., *The Academic Mind* (Glencoe, Ill.: Free Press, 1958).

gists. In consequence, the academic profession often represents social advancement for the individual. Whether this tends to be as true today as perhaps it was thirty and more years ago, we do not know.

The educational preparation for the academic profession is fairly exact. In the various fields of knowledge, known as the disciplines, the prospective scholar is ordinarily expected to prepare himself by graduate study in a leading graduate school culminating in receipt of the Doctor of Philosophy degree. In various professional fields the teacher is expected to have obtained the highest appropriate professional degree awarded for the particular specialization and to have had some experience in the practice of the profession.

As an entrant of the academic profession the faculty member finds that there is a definite hierarchy of rank through which he is expected to advance in his career. The formal ranks are usually those of instructor, assistant professor, associate professor, and professor. An individual college or university will have its own standards for appointment or promotion to each of these ranks. Not every entrant is assured that he or she will achieve the rank of professor, at least in the college or university of his first choice as a place of affiliation. The competition is substantial, and the top rank in the top colleges or universities will go to only a few of all members of the profession.

Perhaps no profession—not even law or medicine —leaves so much determination of effort entirely in the hands of the faculty member himself. We shall note shortly the range of academic decisions made by

the individual faculty member. But the most important decision of all is that involving professional ambitions and standards. How hard the faculty member
works at his field of specialization, whether he gives
primary attention to teaching or to research, how and
what he desires to write and publish, how much he
reads, how much he participates in professional activity and association, how rapidly he seeks to advance
himself professionally—these are largely decisions the
individual faculty member makes for himself with a
minimum amount of pressure from the college or
university itself. To be sure, there are salary and
status incentives to encourage the faculty member, not
to mention of course any family considerations. Yet
by and large the faculty member determines his own
career.

Increasingly the faculty member is a specialist.
A scholar is no longer a botanist, but a botanist specializing in taxonomy, plant genetics, plant ecology,
plant chemistry and cellular structure, plant pathol-
ogy, or various categories of plant life. The political
scientist is a specialist in American political institutions, comparative political institutions, international
relations and law, or political theory. The historian is
a specialist in political history, economic history, or
social and cultural history, as well as a specialist in the
history of particular nations and civilizations at a
particular time period. The physicist is a specialist
in electricity and electronics, acoustics, mechanics,
atomic structure, or solid state physics. The legal
scholar is a specialist in contracts, tax law, antitrust
law, torts, jurisprudence, civil proceedings, criminal

law, or administrative law. In other words, faculty members who share a common discipline or professional field of knowledge may still have only tenuous ties of scholarship one with the other. Scholars may share a broad common concern labeled botany, political science, history, physics, or law, and yet be quite different one from another in the scholarship they profess.

Perhaps faculty members are not more isolated one from another than practitioners of other professions. There is after all a high degree of specialization today in the practice of law and medicine. Yet faculty members in any one college or university possess at best only limited interests in common in so far as their scholarship is concerned.

For most faculty members the closest professional relationships do not occur within a particular academic community but across college or university boundary lines. As a professor of American government at Columbia University, I felt closer ties of kinship with my colleagues in political science at Harvard, Yale, Princeton, Chicago, Michigan, and California than I did with my colleagues in English, physics, or medicine at Columbia. This would be true at most colleges or universities.

It is often said that faculty members have a major loyalty to their discipline or professional field of knowledge rather than to the college or university in which they practice their profession. To a considerable extent this observation is valid. The very nature of the academic profession with its emphasis on specialization promotes this sense of scholarly rather than local or community identity. Moreover, the greatest opportunity for mobility in the profession occurs among individual colleges and universities. The scholar who achieves substantial recognition as teacher, researcher, or both, looks forward to recognition from his fellow scholars and even to an invitation to join a group of colleagues in the few best-known and highest-quality colleges and universities. The degree of mobility thus realized in practice, however, may be less than that commonly supposed.

The faculty member is unique among professional practitioners, however, in that he may pursue his profession only in an academic community. There are today a few nonacademic centers of research where a scholar may carry on his work. But primarily the scholar must be attached to a college or university in order to engage in his instructional and research activity. He is thus bound by ties of convenience and necessity to a particular college or university, even while his scholarly concerns and relationships range far beyond the individual academic community. No matter how he may resent the fact—and such resentment does develop and even grow—the scholar cannot escape the college or university where his work is done.

Thus the scholar's professional endeavor and welfare is inextricably bound up with the welfare of the community of which he is a part, even if often a reluctant part. His scholarship can flourish only to the extent that the college or university flourishes. His only other hope of improvement in status and recognition is to gain a reputation which results in an invitation to join a more flourishing community. In the absence of such an invitation, the scholar must seek his well-being within the confines of the individual college or university where he currently practices his profession. Yet often he senses little if any power in himself personally or in his immediate circle of colleagues to advance his professional status because the advancement of the material well-being of the college or university is beyond his range of activity.

Thus far in this outline of the characteristics of the academic profession we have assumed that scholarship is a profession. In fact, the attributes of a profession are twofold. A profession involves a high degree of knowledge and technical skill utilized by the individual in the service of others. In so far as this attribute is concerned, scholarship in the academic community is clearly a profession. The second attribute of a profession is more complicated. As professions have evolved in Western society they have acquired and articulated a code of ethics. Here the academic profession has been somewhat laggard, for while it has acquired a code of ethics it has been, ironically enough, slow to articulate it.

In practice the academic profession recognizes several important features of a code of ethics. First, the scholar seeks truth and accepts any existing concept of truth only tentatively, recognizing that new concepts may develop from further experimentation, fact gathering, or insight. Secondly, the scholar is tolerant of opposing points of view, even though he may reject the reasoning which is used to uphold them. In the third place, the scholar has a high standard of integrity, believing that the individual must perform his work honestly and to the best of his skill and ability and must clearly acknowledge his intellectual debt to others. In the fourth place, the scholar recognizes limits to his scholarship. He is a specialist in his particular field of study, but the authority of his knowledge does not necessarily extend to other fields of knowledge and does not necessarily provide answers to a variety of practical problems of the everyday world. Finally, the scholar respects the dignity and worth of each individual, whether he be a colleague, fellow worker in a particular academic community, student, or someone beyond the academic community itself.

I believe most if not all faculty members in practically all colleges and universities would willingly and readily acknowledge a code of ethics formulated in some such terms as these. The difficulty in the situation is that the academic profession has developed little if any machinery or tradition of enforcing such standards of behavior. To the extent that they are enforced at all, the task is left to the administration of the academic community rather than being undertaken by the faculty in its corporate capacity.[6] Secondly, the code of ethics just sketched omits any reference to a sense of obligation or responsibility to the college or university in which the scholar practices his profession.

[6] Note the comment on this subject by Henry M. Wriston, *Academic Procession* (New York: Columbia University Press, 1959), pp. 100–101.

Recalling the declaration of William James that teaching is a tyrannical profession, Harold W. Stoke has observed that the college professor "lives in an intellectually frustrating world." [7] He further comments upon the situation in these words: [8]

> During every waking hour the conscientious college professor feels driven by his inadequate preparation for teaching, by the books he has not yet read, the articles not yet written, the ideas not yet clearly formulated. Inside and outside the classroom and the laboratory he carries this guilty load, and it creates for him a sense of strain and indeed a continuity of labor not adequately reflected in the formal teaching schedule. That is why the professor so often feels overworked; he may have a sense of working terribly hard when no one else can see that he is doing anything. Indeed, he *may* be working hard when no one else can see that he is working at all. It is also possible for him to mislead himself into believing that he is working hard when in fact he is only dreading it.

Academic Organization

Every member of the faculty of a college or university has a dual status. He has an individual role and a collegial role. As an individual a faculty member has various important duties to carry out in the

[7] Harold W. Stoke, *The American College President* (New York: Harper & Brothers, 1959), p. 147.

[8] *Ibid.*, pp. 115–116.

performance of his profession.[9] In addition, each member of a faculty has certain duties to perform as part of a company of scholars. Ordinarily these collective duties are performed at three levels of operation: the department, the college or school, and the university. While some individuals tend to have more influence than others, every faculty member has some voice in the determination of matters of academic policy at all three levels of collective or group decision making. The individual contributes to the group process; he is not absorbed by it.

At the departmental and at the college or school level the system for decision making is one of direct democracy. Every person of stated academic rank has an equal voice and vote in the realization of collective action. At the university level the system for decision making may be either direct or representative. The faculty of a university may meet together as a whole and as an academic senate take appropriate actions affecting the general conduct of educational affairs. Except in a very small college or university, much of the actual achievement of an academic consensus rests with committees. Reports from committees will usually be accepted by the entire faculty membership of a college and by the entire faculty membership of a

[9] Although I use the masculine gender here and elsewhere as a matter of convenience, I would not want anyone to suppose that I think of faculty members as being only of the male sex. I would acknowledge both the presence and the substantial service of women members of the faculties in various colleges and universities.

university. The alternative will ordinarily be no decision or action at all. In their collective capacity a college or school faculty and a university faculty will criticize committee reports, occasionally modify a provision of general interest, or even move to recommit some matter for further committee deliberation. In these respects a college faculty and a university faculty are much like a legislative chamber as a whole.

In some instances at the university level it is not feasible as a matter of size for the entire faculty to meet as a collegial whole. Instead a faculty council or another such deliberative body will represent the various college and school faculties and will decide policy questions of university-wide interest in the academic realm.

It may be well to acknowledge that in some colleges and universities other levels of cooperative or group faculty concern have been established besides those of the department, the school or college, and the university. In some instances a department may have a research center or research project attached to it involving several but not all departmental faculty members. In others a research or other activity may be attached to a college or school, bringing together persons from various departments. In still other circumstances at the university level a special research center or instructional service may be established, bringing together faculty members from various colleges and schools. Usually, these departmental, college and school, and university agencies are located at the organizational level necessary to associate those individuals of a common interest. Thus, if a center for radiation research is to be established, it will probably be an agency of university level since it might seek to associate in a common cause certain faculty members from the biological sciences, the physical sciences, medicine, law, and engineering.

Sometimes it may be thought desirable to group various departments of a college of arts and sciences in a division of physical science or a division of the social sciences. Presumably this would not be done unless there was some active educational program for several departments to join in operating. Groupings of departments and even of schools have very little utility unless there is something specific in the way of a curriculum or program of studies for a joint enterprise to fulfill.

Increasingly today there are various educational services available to colleges and schools and departments which for reasons of convenience are centralized at the university level. A radio and television broadcasting service is a ready example, as well as an audio-visual service, a library, a museum, and similar activities. In general the organizational complexity in academic matters of a college or university will depend upon the size and scope of educational programs offered. The greater the variety of educational programs, the more complicated will be the structure of academic organization.

More and more some kind of formal organizational arrangement is being employed in a college or university in order to bring together persons of different departments having some common interest in a problem area, such as American studies, urban affairs, or research on the aged. Research techniques are now so specialized that groups of scholars must be brought together. The individual scholar more and more depends upon association with others in both instructional and research activities.

Regardless of the specific issues of academic organization which may arise, universities commonly confront two or three perplexing difficulties. One of these is the relationship between undergraduate and graduate instruction. Another is the relationship between the disciplines and professional fields of instruction. A third is the relationship between instruction and research. Seldom are these problems resolved in organizational terms to the satisfaction of all members of a faculty or to all elements of the academic community. We shall comment about these difficulties and about organizational solutions to them as we proceed.

The Individual Faculty Member

The basic unit in the educational process is the individual faculty member. Upon the instructor-scholar rests the primary authority and responsibility for the conduct of the academic enterprise. Like the lawyer and the doctor, the professor works alone. He may look to others for advice and guidance, he may operate within the context of departmental and college and university policy, and he may have as resources only what is made available to him through budgetary allotments. Yet the professor is still singly in charge of his classroom. Here he is in authority,

and few if any will try to control or direct his behavior.

The faculty member may be assigned a course to
teach. If he is an older and well-known member of the
academic staff he may decide for himself what subject
he wishes to teach. Only under the most extraordinary
circumstances of college or university impoverishment would a faculty member be asked to teach a subject for which he had not prepared himself by education and experience. In ordinary circumstances a
faculty member is recruited by a department to teach
a specialized discipline or profession or subdivision
thereof. To the extent that he is an instructor competent in his subject-matter area, effective in communication, and proper in personal conduct, he will
continue his teaching over a considerable period of
time.

Within the framework of the courses offered by
his department, the faculty member determines for
himself course content and scope, instructional procedure, and expectations of student achievement. The
outline of subject matter to be covered in the course,
the selection of a textbook and other readings, the
assignment of projects and papers to be undertaken
by students, the timing of the instructional process
(within the limits of the college or university calendar
and schedule), the use of lecture as against the discussion method of instruction, the employment of visual
materials—these are all matters left to the discretion
of the individual faculty member. Furthermore, the
entire process of student evaluation is another vital
responsibility of the professor. He may use standard-

ized or nonstandardized tests, he may use one or many tests, and he may grade on a curve or fix certain absolute standards of performance. The grade or mark of achievement for the student rests with the judgment of the individual faculty member.

To be sure, here again departmental decisions may enter in, especially in the so-called "introductory" course. Textbooks, readings, visual materials, and testing practice may then be decided by the department, since all or most members of the department may be involved in teaching the introductory course. In his specialized field of learning, however, where he shares his endeavor with perhaps no other colleague, the faculty member is on his own.

In the academic profession today there is a good deal of discussion about the adequate preparation of the instructor to fulfill his instructional duties. Should it be assumed that any person who masters a field of learning is thereby automatically qualified to communicate effectively and to evaluate students fairly? Some have answered this in the negative and have tried by means of courses in the learning process and in tests and measurements to advance the professional competence of the individual instructor. Some have wanted older and experienced instructors to observe the young and new instructor in the classroom. From such observation may come advice and assistance in improving the instructor's ability to communicate and to judge student performance. Neither of these efforts has gained substantial adherence or practice in the academic profession.

At graduate levels of teaching the faculty member

may work more and more with individual students rather than with groups. Usually there are master's essays and doctoral dissertations to be read with care and judged on the basis of the merit of each student's performance. Sometimes there are research procedures and results of a student project to be closely observed. On occasion a committee of two or three persons in a department may pass judgment upon the performance of a student, but frequently a single faculty member judges the work of the most advanced graduate and professional students.

It must not be thought, however, that the individual faculty member within his classroom is subject to no limit upon his authority. The instructor is continually being evaluated by his students. And this evaluation over a period of time may be surprisingly accurate. The faculty member acquires a certain reputation for being a good lecturer, for being an exciting actor, for expressing unusual points of view, for being a stimulating discussion leader, for being a helpful assistant to young researchers, for being an easy "grader," for being an exacting taskmaster. These reactions are evident in the quality and number of students attracted by the faculty member. There is a danger, of course, that student evaluation may not be sufficiently well informed to be reliable. For example, many students come to appreciate the qualities of a faculty member only after they have begun to practice their own profession. In this situation alumni evaluation may serve as a counterweight to student reaction.

As a scholar a man's performance is subject to the critical scrutiny of his own peers. Each published

article, each book review, each research project recorded, each participation in professional discussions,
each book—all are carefully observed and remembered. No faculty member can escape the judgment of
his colleagues in a particular college or university and
in the scholarly world at large.

Student and scholarly assessment of the individual finds its way into the record of promotion and
salary increases. The evaluation need not be formalized; it may not be systematically evidenced by a rat-
ing sheet. This does not mean that the assessment is
any the less important or reliable. The poor teacher
and the poor scholar are usually well known on any
faculty. Occasionally an individual may feel that his
qualities have not been fairly judged by peers and by
deans. If there is a real measure of unfairness, the
individual may seek a different academic affiliation;
he may move to another college or university. With
the great demand which colleges and universities now
experience for faculty members, this safeguard is very
real.

Thus the faculty member may be an individual
in the performance of his activity, but he is not an
isolated person freed from responsibility to his profession, to his students, and to his immediate colleagues. The faculty member controls his work but
the result is subject to continuing evaluation.

The Department

In every college or university the customary first
grouping of faculty members is the department. It is

the department which brings together all persons with a common subject-matter interest. It is the department which expresses the common professional allegiance of the faculty.

Under the guidance or leadership of a chairman or executive officer, each department has a number of vital decisions to make. Ordinarily it is the department as a group which decides the general scope and specialization of subject matter to be undertaken in the course offerings. Ordinarily it is the department which determines the individual member who shall be invited to join the group, within the staffing limits established by the dean or the president of the college or university. Ordinarily it is the department collectively or through consultation of its senior members which decides whom to recommend for promotion in rank and for increases in salary. These recommendations may be reviewed by another group of academic personnel, but departmental recommendation is usually a vital first step in the process.

A department ordinarily determines both what courses it shall provide its students and what sequence and number of courses shall be required for a "major." These decisions are subject to further review at the college and university level, but they are generally accepted without great questioning. The department is expected only to keep its demand upon the total time allowance of the college or school within the limits of a general scheme of distribution and concentration of courses.

Sometimes a department or a committee of a department may be involved in deciding important questions concerning students. There may be scholarship and fellowship applications to review and decide. There may be the question whether a particular student should be given advanced credit for studies previously completed, whether to admit a student to an honors program, whether to graduate a student with honors, or whether to admit a student to various levels of specialized study.

A department is necessarily involved in a variety of relations with other departments. Just how close these relationships may be will depend upon the policy and structural arrangements of a college or university. If it is the policy to encourage interdisciplinary instruction and research, then fairly close relationships may be developed between the departments involved. If the organizational pattern calls for close working relationships, then collaboration may be the price of participation in a common enterprise.

As an illustration of departmental cooperation, let me cite a program of Russian studies. If a university is to launch a fairly comprehensive effort to educate American students in Russian culture and society, it will have to bring together scholars in Russian language, Russian literature, Russian history, Russian culture and society, Russian government, and Russian economy. Russian language and literature may involve a single department, but otherwise the historian will probably come from a history department, the sociologist from a sociology department, the government specialist from a political science department, and the economist from an economics department. Each will have in common his ability to speak and read Russian and his specialization in the application of his subject-matter competence to a particular society. Yet the Russian historian is first an historian.

If a university wishes to establish an institute of Russian studies, it may ask each of several departments representing these various disciplines to staff courses dealing with its subject-matter competence as focused upon Russia. In this way an organizational pattern is created whereby a number of departments may work together toward a common educational objective.

The same sort of arrangement may occur in research activities. For example, a research program concerned with missiles may bring together chemists, physicists, mathematicians, astronomers, engineers, and even medical personnel and biologists. Each discipline and each professional field of knowledge will have to contribute their special competencies to the common enterprise. The individual faculty member continues his basic allegiance to and status in the department which represents his special competence.

These interrelationships of scholars may be directed or supervised to some degree from above the department level. But collaboration among departments in instruction and research tends to be first of all a voluntary matter. And there often is a great deal of informal collaboration which never appears directly in joint or interdependent course offerings or in an actual continuing research program.

The expansion of research activity within universities has brought one important innovation at the departmental level in recent years. To some extent many departments and universities have had to recognize two classes of personnel—the regular faculty member and the research faculty member. Perhaps the only real difference between the two arises from the academic practice of tenure. The regular faculty member enjoys the privilege of tenure; the research faculty member does not. The differentiation is supposed to recognize differences in financial support. The federal government, the largest single source of funds for university research, might at any time decide not to provide the necessary income. The research faculty member might then be relieved from his contract of employment. Yet a college or university might also suffer a loss of student or endowment or gift income and have to reduce its regular staff.

Furthermore, the research faculty member is supposed to give all his time to research, but he often works with graduate students and other faculty members and is frequently in demand as a lecturer. The real as opposed to the imagined difference between a regular and a research faculty member is not so great as is sometimes imagined. It is a matter of emphasis or of degree rather than of substance.

In our largest universities with the most extensive research programs the departmental absorption of research personnel has created some tensions. Those members of a department not actively engaged in research may resent the "new breed" of research specialists developing among them. They may dislike their concentration upon research, their guaranteed employment for twelve months of the year, their better compensation (when this occurs). Moreover, the very number of these research specialists may appear to pose a threat to departmental domination by an "old guard." It is no easy task for deans or university academic leaders to try to adjust such situations.

These comments may seem to suggest a belief on my part that all research and instructional activities should be related formally or informally to the departmental organization of a university. The impression is correct. Even where separate research institutes are established at the university level of operation, I believe strongly that all such research endeavors should be closely related to departments. In this way staff members have a home base in the specialized field of scholarship whose knowledge and techniques are being applied to general or specific research problems. Moreover, an interchange of students and faculty participation in research and instruction can be helpful to all concerned. If a research activity is to be organized as a part of a university and not separate from it, then the activity ought to operate, I believe, as an integral part of the entire university community, and this means close departmental ties.

It is at the departmental level of academic organization where conflict especially occurs between undergraduate and graduate instruction. No university seems to have resolved the problem of achieving a balance of talent at the departmental level devoted to both undergraduate and graduate instruction. When graduate programs are extensive and enroll high-quality students, academic prestige attaches to this activity. Often the faculty member has fewer students and fewer formal courses at the graduate than at the undergraduate level. Often he receives more encouragement and assistance for his own research program. There is a real tendency for the outstanding members of a faculty to prefer graduate to undergraduate instruction.

The prevailing pattern of academic organization prescribes that a department shall offer both undergraduate and graduate courses. Sometimes the burden of instruction for undergraduate students falls to graduate assistants or to young instructors just beginning their academic careers. Sometimes senior members of a department may be persuaded to teach one undergraduate course but otherwise to avoid student advising and other undergraduate chores.

Because of a feeling that departments are not evidencing a proper degree of interest in their undergraduate programs, some universities have tried the device of separating faculties into undergraduate and graduate groups, and even of establishing new departments in the undergraduate college. In my judgment both arrangements have their faults. The persons recruited for undergraduate instruction are likely to feel cut off from their colleagues in their disciplines and to believe that their own academic careers have been somehow curtailed. The great ambition of the faculty member in the undergraduate college is likely to be to see how quickly he can gain promotion to the graduate faculty. And graduate faculties unconnected with undergraduate study grow out of touch with the previous preparation of their students. Each department in a university has to work out for itself how best to meet both undergraduate and graduate instructional demands. This is a decision of major academic importance.

A final word should be said about the departmental chairman. His is a vital position in academic affairs. He must guide his colleagues in their decision making. He must settle or adjust disputes among departmental members. He must place departmental objectives above those of any individual member. He must serve as a link between department and school or college. He must build for long-term growth and eminence in departmental reputation among other colleges and universities.

The department chairman may be appointed by the president upon nomination by a dean, or he may be elected by the members of the department. Each selection process has its faults and its virtues. Appointment after careful consultation with members of the department seems the preferable practice. The term of office may be indefinite or fixed. Some rotation seems desirable in most circumstances. A department chairman may stay too long.

It must be evident from this discussion that departments are a very important element of academic organization. They provide scholarly association and the basic group for decision making about fundamental issues of instruction and research.

The College and School

Beyond the department is the college or school. Ordinarily a dean occupies the formal position of leadership for the college or school. Even so, the faculty collectively and through committees is heavily involved in the decision-making process.

Sometimes a university reserves the designation "college" for the college of arts and sciences and the designation "school" for all other instructional units. Sometimes the term "college" applies to all units of joint undergraduate and graduate instruction, such as a college of education, a college of engineering, and a college of agriculture, in addition to a college of arts and sciences. In this system the label "school" is then reserved for professional schools enrolling college graduates, such as a school of law, a school of medicine, a school of theology, or a graduate school. Sometimes an intermixture of the designations may be utilized almost indiscriminately.

In some schools, as in a law school, departmental jurisdiction may be relatively unimportant or even nonexistent; the role of department and of school may thus be merged. The instructional staff of the school becomes in effect a department as well. This is not often the case, however, except in relatively small and homogeneous instructional units known as schools. Usually the college or school represents an aggregation of departments.

Sometimes, especially in a college of arts and sciences, a "division" form of organization may be attempted. A division of the humanities, a division of the biological sciences, a division of the social sciences, and a division of the physical sciences may be established. At the University of Chicago, under the leadership of Chancellor Robert M. Hutchins, such divisions became major components of the university in which schools, colleges, and departments were constituent elements. Usually a division pattern has little meaning unless some definite decisions about course offerings and staffing of instruction have been assigned to these groupings.

At the college or school level the basic decision which must be made is one of general scope of the curriculum as a whole. First, there is the decision to be made whether the degree program shall require one, two, three, four, or more years. There are also decisions to be made about the number of credit hours of course work to require for a degree or various degrees, together with a pattern of distribution among various subject-matter fields. In a large college or school of several departments, such decisions are apt to represent a compromise among departmental points of view. A certain amount of logrolling among departments is not unknown; one department expects its ideas of a desirable curriculum to be respected when it in turn respects the ideas of other departments.

The college or school is also an important level of review in matters of departmental curriculum construction, appointment and promotion of personnel, salary and other budget needs, student advising, and requirements for physical facilities. Sometimes all or part of these subjects are referred to standing or special committees by a dean. Sometimes the dean may seek only such informal consultation with influential members of the faculty as he deems desirable.

The faculty of a college or a school usually meets

from time to time as a collective body to express its official and formal point of view. This may be quite formal indeed, with the major policy decisions on curriculum, student advising, and even budget needs being taken within committees. On the other hand, the college or school faculty may debate various matters of academic policy at some length and in great detail. Much depends upon size, tradition, and the quality of leadership within the faculty.

Usually it is the faculty of a college or school which decides when students have fulfilled all requirements for a degree. The record keeping of the college or university may largely determine this fact, but nonetheless a formal voting of all degrees is still customary in many academic groups.

A word should be added about the role of the dean. His leadership has been called a leadership of equals, and even of academic "middle management." [10] In a sense the dean does stand in the middle of the process by which scarce resources are allocated to the instructional parts of a university. The dean is expected to be the spokesman of the faculty to the administration of a university, and at the same time the outpost of the administration in conveying an understanding of general university points of view. The dean reviews the personnel practices of departments. He formulates the budget for his college or school and participates in its administration.

[10] Harlan Cleveland, "The Dean's Dilemma: Leadership of Equals," *Public Administration Review*, vol. 20 (Winter, 1960), p. 22.

Usually the dean is more than this. He does not issue orders to departments or faculty members, but he stands as a symbol of their collegial responsibility. He is a reminder to all the faculty members of a college or school of their common purpose and common interest. To the extent that he can articulate this common purpose and can win adherents to it, the dean has fulfilled an essential role in the academic process.

The University

The point of view of the university as a whole in academic matters is represented by the faculty as a whole and by the leadership of the faculty. Sometimes, especially in a large university, it is not practical for the faculty to meet as one general, deliberative body. In these circumstances there may be a senate, which is representative in character, or a council on which elected representatives of the faculty sit. The leadership of the faculty on academic matters is usually vested in a president and his associate, a vice president (or provost) for academic affairs.

The university-wide role of a faculty in a large university is not easy to define. Obviously the faculty as a whole has a number of common concerns. These tend to center in the welfare and operation of the university as an environment of learning. The faculty is interested in the use of the resources of the university. The faculty is interested in the preservation of academic freedom. The faculty is interested in actions which tend to establish or diminish the academic reputation, the standards of quality of the university. The faculty is interested in the academic objectives of the university and how they are to be realized.

The problem arises when efforts are made to express these interests in concrete terms of organization and decision making. For example, should a university-wide committee be established to review promotion, tenure, and salary practices, as well as policies? Should a university-wide committee be set up to participate in the budget process? Should a university-wide committee be set up to review decisions which appear to affect academic freedom and academic integrity? And if such committees are established, what actual power other than a general power of criticism shall be vested in them?

Part of the complexity arises from the nature of academic leadership in the university. Part of the complexity arises, too, from the necessity of so many day-to-day decisions which must be made promptly and which affect the entire university. Faculty leadership is usually vested in a president and an associate (vice president, provost, or dean of faculties). These leaders are not elected by the faculty; they are appointed by the board of trustees. I shall have more to say about this later. If their leadership is to be effective, however, at least two minimum prerequisites are essential. First, a president and his associate should have had faculty experience. Secondly, the faculty through a consultative committee should have had some voice in the selection process of the persons to fill these positions.

The president and his associate must be careful

to represent the best interests of the faculty as a whole if they are to be in fact faculty leaders. At the same time their administrative role (to be considered later) requires them to represent also the best interests of the university as a whole. The interests of the faculty and the interests of the university are not necessarily identical, although they are of course highly interrelated.

The president and his academic associate will usually work closely with a council of deans and other administrative officers. This group is apt to make the decisions which involve faculty interests. To the extent that such a group does in effect represent faculty points of view or is considerate of those points of view, this arrangement may be satisfactory in practice. But a group of this kind is often apt to forget, or to fail to distinguish, when it is making a decision preponderantly one of academic concern and when it is making a decision preponderantly one of administrative concern.

Faculty members often desire an elected consultative committee which will be kept informed about developing policies and decisions of university-wide interest. Such a committee can be highly useful if presidents and their academic associates will make appropriate use of them. A consultative committee is not a decision-making committee, but at least it is available as a representative expression of faculty points of view.

In some universities there are a certain number of decisions which must be made on a university-wide basis. These may include the number, scope, and content of degree programs; the general enactment of student-conduct regulations; the voting of degrees; the determination of recipients of honorary degrees; the general policies on promotion and tenure; the approval of curricula and even courses for various schools and colleges; the administration of student aid; the administration of student admission; and the handling of appeals for exceptions from academic regulations. Some of these matters may be handled by direct faculty vote. Some may be handled by formal faculty approval upon recommendation of faculty committees. Some may be handled by an elected council which also includes academic officers.

Perhaps the two most troublesome issues in practice are promotions and budgeting. I shall discuss the budget process in a later chapter. In so far as promotions are concerned, there is a need for a university-wide committee to make certain that to some extent common standards are observed on a university-wide basis. The question at issue generally is whether this committee should be appointed or elected. I am disposed to believe that appointed committees are somewhat more generous in their attitudes on the subject of promotion, and for this reason alone tend to favor the appointed committee. If a faculty so insists, however, there can be an elected committee.

In any event, there are faculty decisions which must be made on a university-wide basis. These may be made through direct faculty meetings or through a wide variety of representative committees or through both devices. The process of decision making necessarily must include academic officers who are appointed as well as elected, since these officers have a full-time responsibility for seeing that faculty interests are duly administered.

The Disciplines and the Professions

In every university, and even in the separately established college, there is conflict between those of the faculty who are members of a discipline and those who are members of a profession. The departments representing disciplines usually comprise a faculty of arts and sciences, or a college of arts and sciences, providing both undergraduate and graduate instruction. The disciplines represent the broad subject-matter areas of knowledge: language, literature, philosophy, history, economics, political science, sociology, psychology, botany, zoology, physiology, geology, mathematics, astronomy, chemistry, and physics. It is in these subject-matter areas that much "pure" research is carried on to advance knowledge.

The professional departments usually comprise the professional colleges and schools where the educational objective is more narrowly directed to instruction of students in the technique and skill of applying knowledge to practical problems of everyday life. Such professional instruction may be solely at the graduate level, as in law, medicine, and theology. Such professional instruction may be largely at the undergraduate level, as is the case with agriculture, nursing, fine arts, and veterinary medicine. And increasingly professional instruction may be both undergraduate and graduate, as in engineering, teacher education, and business administration.

The disciplines tend to regard themselves as the elite of the university faculty and to look down upon their professional colleagues. Partly this attitude reflects a belief that professional faculties are too much concerned with technique and method in professional practice and too little concerned with basic knowledge. Partly this attitude reflects a belief that professional faculties are largely composed of poor scholars, that is, of persons with an inadequate mastery of a subject-matter field. It is often pointed out that great advances in medicine, for example, result from the research effort of chemists and biologists rather than of doctors. And there is just enough truth in the statement to create embarrassment for the medical profession.

In recent years one of the outstanding developments in higher education in the United States has been the increasingly high degree of collaboration between the disciplines and the professions. This is evident in large measure, to cite a single illustration, in engineering. There was a time when the disciplines of chemistry and physics were rudimentary at best; and the engineering profession could concentrate attention upon practical problems of construction, the generation and distribution of electricity, mining and metallurgy, and mechanical power upon the basis of practical experience and a few simple rules of thumb. Today this is all changed. The knowledge of chemistry and physics has grown immensely; the practical problems of energy and metallurgy are far more complicated than ever before. The result is that the physical sciences and the now so-called "engineering sciences" have come close together indeed. The only difference many can find at present is to insist that engineers are concerned with economics—with the cost of various forms of scientific application to practical problems in such areas as the production of energy, missiles, and electronic computers.

A part of this growing collaboration has come about as the result of the increased competence in a discipline on the part of many professional faculty members. The faculty of a school of business administration finds itself engaged in research in economics and social psychology. The faculty of a medical school finds itself engaged in research in genetics or physics. The faculty of a school of education finds itself engaged in research not only in social psychology but also in economics and public finance. More and more, members of the professional faculties have advanced their competence as scholars in various disciplines; and more and more, scholars have been drawn into the faculties of professional schools.

The problem of relationship between the disciplines and the professions remains a troublesome one at almost all large universities. At the University of Pittsburgh the experiment has been tried of organizing a College of the Academic Disciplines to provide staffing for the undergraduate college of liberal arts, the graduate school, and many of the professional schools.[11] Most universities have not been willing to make so formal an arrangement, preferring a variety of relationships. Some professional schools, as already indicated, seek to recruit certain faculty members from the disciplines. Some professional schools encourage faculty members to continue their own education to the point of mastery of the subject-matter content and research procedure of a discipline. Some universities encourage collaboration between the disciplines and the professions by joint appointments, by joint courses or joint curricula, and by joint research activities.

There continues to be an essential difference between the disciplines and the professional schools. The disciplines concentrate upon advancing subject-matter competence in a specialized field of learning. The professional schools concentrate upon advancing the competence of persons to solve practical problems utilizing all available and applicable fields of knowledge. Let us use as an illustration of the difference between the disciplines and the professions this very field of large-scale organization and the administrative process. As disciplines, political science, economics, sociology, and psychology have all been concerned in some degree with organization and administration as part of government, economic enterprise, social institutions, and human behavior. But in a school of public administration or in a school of business adminis-

[11] Edward H. Litchfield, "Organization in Large American Universities: The Faculties," *Journal of Higher Education,* vol. 30 (October, 1959), p. 353.

tration the points of view of all these disciplines must be brought together to focus upon the practical problems of organizing and operating governmental administrative agencies and business corporations. The disciplines and the professions are both essential to our concept of higher education in American society, and some means for their fruitful collaboration must be found in each university.

The Academic Environment

As I have suggested, the faculty member as an individual finds himself more concerned with his subject-matter discipline or professional area than with the welfare of the particular college or university in which he practices his profession. This does not mean that he is completely indifferent to his academic environment. The contrary is the case. The faculty member has several definite expectations in his relationship to the college or university of which he is a part.

First of all, every faculty member expects that the system of organization and operation in a college or university will recognize the importance of the role of the faculty member and provide him with a status of dignity and consideration. The faculty member does not think of himself as an employee of the college or university. In particular, he resents any suggestion that his relations to a dean, a vice president for academic affairs, and a president involve supervisory authority. The supposed power of a president to give orders to a faculty member does not exist, or will not long be tolerated in any college or university of intellectual quality.

The faculty member is an individual professional practitioner of scholarship. His learning, his ability as a teacher, his competence in research cannot be ordered by a dean or other official of the college or university. These qualities can be exercised only as the individual is moved by pride in himself and his profession to make the most of them. The faculty member wants his status recognized. He wants it appreciated and paid its due respect.

Secondly, the faculty member expects to be provided appropriate facilities for the practice of his profession and proper remuneration for his services. Difficulty arises because it is not easy to define "appropriate facilities" or "proper remuneration" and because the individual faculty member is largely dependent upon the college or university for both. As an individual professional practitioner, the faculty member does not make a charge directly to his clientele for services rendered. He does not rent or own office or laboratory space. He does not hire and pay instructional assistants, a secretary, or clerks. All the facilities for the practice of his profession and the remuneration are provided through the college or university of which he is a part. The profession of scholarship is socialized in our society.

We need not stop here to discuss either the salary or the plant problems of higher education. It is sufficient to repeat that the academic profession as a profession does not determine either its level of professional compensation or the adequacy of the physical facilities available for instruction and research. The academic community of a college or university as a whole does not make these decisions. The institution of higher education must depend upon its status as a religious, welfare, governmental, and economic enterprise in order to obtain the financial resources for its operation. The faculty in any particular college or university may help in enlarging its resources. In general, however, the academic community as a whole, not the faculty as a profession, determines available economic resources. The faculty member expects appropriate facilities and proper remuneration, but often this expectation is disappointed.

Thirdly, the faculty member expects freedom in which to pursue his profession of scholarship. He expects the academic community to protect his privilege to instruct students and to advance knowledge without external pressure and without the requirement of social approval. To be sure, this privilege entails obligations as well. Academic freedom is meaningful only within the academic community. The freedom of the classroom or of the laboratory does not necessarily carry over to freedom in the economic and political market place. Here the scholar takes his chances with all others in society. Here the scholar is simply another citizen. Yet it is not easy to draw a line between classroom and public discussion, between laboratory and economic competition. But the faculty member expects the institution of higher education in some way to protect his freedom of scholarship.

I must say that these expectations do not seem un-

reasonable, given the nature of higher education and
its importance. At the same time, these expectations
create tensions within a particular college or university and for the whole institution of higher education.
I shall say more about these tensions at the conclusion
of this essay.

One other observation may be justified. It is a
comment often made by administrative officers and
others who have had occasion to watch faculty behavior at close hand. The individual faculty member and,
even more, the collective faculty body are essentially
quite conservative in their attitudes on academic matters. The contrast is notable between the faculty member as a scholar and the faculty member as a professional practitioner of scholarship.

As a scholar the faculty member is constantly
exploring new ideas and seeking to enlarge the knowledge and skill of students. The scholar welcomes
change in the knowledge available to him and promotes change in the knowledge held by students. The
scholar may even be quite critical because men of
power in economic affairs, government, and elsewhere
do not embrace change upon the basis of a growing
knowledge in the conduct of their own enterprises.
On the other hand, the scholar wants to be left alone
in the conduct of the academic enterprise. He does
not welcome innovation in instructional procedures,
in instructional arrangements, or in the organization
and operation of a college or university. Social change
in higher education often comes slowly, as in other
institutions. The scholar is a conservative in his attitude toward and appreciation of the academic process.

The academic profession is unique in many of its characteristics. We have tried here to sketch some of its peculiar features. At the same time, the academic profession is the very heart of the academic enterprise. The faculty is a vital constituent group of the academic community. It is not a subordinate level of workers operating under a structure of hierarchical authority. Faculty members exercise individual and collective responsibility for the conduct of the learning and research process in a college or university.

Nonetheless, by the nature of the academic community, the faculty cannot be all-powerful. There are other constituent groups to be considered. These too have an important role in the affairs of higher education.

Chapter 4

Students

IN A WELL-KNOWN BIT of American folklore, the educational process has been pictured as a log with the instructor at one end and the student at the other. Whatever may be the various bits of homely wisdom drawn from the analogy, at least this much is without question: Education means more than a scholar. It requires also a student. It is the student who helps complete the process of preserving, transmitting, and advancing knowledge.

In the United States, students represent a wide variety of economic and social backgrounds, a wide variety of intellectual abilities, a wide variety of motivations for learning. This circumstance is both the joy and the despair of higher education in our country. We undertake to provide an opportunity for college or undergraduate education to a larger proportion of our youth than does any other nation in the world. In the process we have had to modify our educational objectives and our educational procedures.

We must acknowledge that in the United States the goal of higher education is not simply to prepare an intellectual elite or to provide a relatively small proportion of individuals to practice the most highly intellectualized professions, such as theology, law, medicine, engineering, and higher education itself. Rather, we have enlarged the number of professions and recognized new fields of educational endeavor, such as elementary and secondary education, nursing, dietetics and food management, interior and clothing design, art and architecture, accounting, business administration, market research, product research and development, economic analysis, dramatic art, and others. Nor do we necessarily expect that every young person acquiring a specialized competency in one of these areas of interest will necessarily become a professional practitioner. The interest may be only an amateur one providing continuing individual satisfaction. Or a person may express his or her competence within the realm of the family or in voluntary community service.

We must not overlook either the role of higher education in promoting social mobility and in providing a symbol of social achievement. Traditionally, one great objective of higher education has been to provide opportunity to youth of talent regardless of current social and economic status. In an open society such as ours in the United States where individual effort and ability have won notable rewards, higher education has been especially and increasingly important in providing an avenue for the individual to rise from one to another social and economic class. Because change in social status has so often been attributed to the benefits of higher education, a college education has become one of the status symbols of our society. To provide our children an opportunity for higher education is an evidence of our own social and economic achievement as parents.

Society in the United States has a stake in higher education. A large element of college-educated persons has seemed important to the functioning of a political system in which ultimate political power rests with a numerous electorate. A large element of college-educated persons has seemed important to the preservation of higher education as an institution. A large element of college-educated persons has seemed important to the realization of educational opportunity for individual and varied talents. And a large element of college-educated persons has seemed important to staff the work of our society and to advance our economic growth.

All this background so briefly outlined must be kept in mind as we discuss the student in American higher education. Any generalization about students must allow for considerable variety in their backgrounds, their abilities, their motivations. Some students are concerned to achieve a rigorous intellectual preparation for highly specialized and highly exacting professions. Some are concerned to prepare for less demanding roles in our society. Others are almost indifferent to any intellectual accomplishment. Widely varying motivations have brought them all within the reach of higher education.

The Student as a Learner

Learning is individual. A group is never educated. Only individuals learn. A group process may promote individual learning. This is indeed what a college or university does: It provides a group process for individual learning. The student, moreover, is not just a passive recipient of knowledge. He must do more than listen and repeat for himself the learning propounded by a scholar. The student must be able to discuss and evaluate knowledge, retain knowledge, and practice the utilization of knowledge. The learning process involves many procedures.

A college or university operates in groups: groups of students in a classroom, in a library, in a laboratory, in a residence hall, in some other collective body. Such groups are necessary as a matter of convenience and economy. Such groups may stimulate the intellectual effort of the individual. It is still the individual who listens, reads, discusses, experiments, and practices. It is still the individual who learns.

The student is also a person with drives, with needs, with goals which go beyond the formal learning process of higher education. The college or university is concerned with knowledge. It is thus concerned with only a part of life, that part in which knowledge is important as personal satisfaction and social utility. But the student who participates in the process of learning is a person with emotions and ambitions. He has a life to live, like everyone else, which moves beyond the realm of knowledge. No frustration is so great to the faculty and to the administrative officers of a university as to witness a student's indifference to his opportunity to learn. In the academic community, the first goal, the supreme commitment, is to reason and learning. The student often has not yet reached that point of commitment.

There is probably a great difference in this matter of commitment between the undergraduate and the graduate student. The undergraduate is younger, just emerged from the shelter of home, just beginning to experiment with maturity. The undergraduate is often less certain of his goals. In the United States he may even be experimenting with learning, trying to determine whether he wants to make the effort to complete four years of college work. The graduate student, on the other hand, is older, further removed from parental concern, across the threshold of adult maturity. He is more certain of his goals; he is beyond the stage of experimentation with learning. He has completed four years of college work; he has obtained a college degree; he is continuing his education in order to complete preparation for one of the higher professions. He is apt to be married, especially today.

It is very important in any discussion of students to differentiate between the undergraduate and the graduate student. The undergraduate has more problems as a person—or at least *seems* to have more such problems—and less commitment to learning. The graduate student has fewer problems as a person, or at least he has found how to subordinate these problems to a major goal: the acquisition of learning and skill. The graduate is no longer an apprentice; he is a journeyman in the craft of knowledge, ready to serve closely and effectively with his master teacher. In any event, this is the ideal. But in this discussion our attention will be concentrated upon the undergraduate, and our observations are only indirectly if at all applicable to the graduate student in the arts and sciences or in the professions.

The Campus

In most discussions of higher education in America there are often extensive contrasts drawn between the privately sponsored and the publicly sponsored college or university, the small college versus the large college or university, the liberal arts college versus the professional school, the college or university of high quality and substantial prestige versus the college or university of lower quality and lesser prestige. All these contrasts have some meaning, although it is easy to exaggerate the actual differences. This is especially true when trying to draw distinctions between the privately and the publicly sponsored college or university.

In the discussion of students, however, there is another contrast which is probably far more important than any of those just mentioned. The role of the undergraduate student in the academic community varies greatly, depending upon whether the college or university he attends is residential or commuter in relationship to student life. In the residential college or university, housing of students is an important part of academic life. The student lives away from home. He has gotten away from his parental roof and surveillance. The college or university to some degree must substitute its supervision for that of the parents. More than this, the college or university must seek to promote or encourage social activity by students which complements but does not compete with intellectual activity.

The commuter college or university does not undertake to provide housing for its students. The student ordinarily lives at home with his parents. Parental supervision thus continues during the undergraduate years. The college or university assumes little if any responsibility for student social conduct under these circumstances. To some extent there may be a social program at the college or university to provide an opportunity for students living at home to attend a few social events with persons of their own age and general interest. Such a social program does not have to be particularly extensive.

The college or university with a commuting student body does have its special problems. The home environment may not encourage learning by the student. The student's need to work may interfere with his study. The student may be so distracted by various aspects of urban living that he gives less and less attention to learning. The student may miss that part of the educational process which does promote learning by the close association of students and scholars and by the practice of student group activity. In various ways and through various counselors, the college or university with a commuting student population endeavors to overcome its limitations.

Universities located in a large city may be either of the commuter or residential type. Harvard in Cambridge, Yale in New Haven, Brown in Providence, Vanderbilt in Nashville, and Emory in Atlanta are residential universities. Boston University, New York University, the City University of New York, Temple University, the University of Cincinnati, St. Louis University, Wayne State University, the University of California in Los Angeles are primarily commuter universities. Sometimes large state universities in major cities like the Ohio State University, the University of Minnesota, and the University of Washington depend in great measure upon rooming houses to provide housing for students close to, or some distance from, the campus.

A university or college located in a small town must provide housing for its student body from necessity. This means that the college or university must also encourage and supervise an especially extensive social life, since there is no surrounding city in which student life can be absorbed by the anonymity of a metropolis. Many of the leading liberal arts colleges of the United States are located in small towns, as are a few universities, such as Princeton, Pennsylvania State, North Carolina, and Mississippi.

A great deal of difference in the role of the student body in the academic community therefore depends upon these factors: the proportion of full-time undergraduate students to the total student body of a university; the residential as opposed to the commuter type of college or university; the large (or even middle-sized) city location as opposed to the small-town location. As I have already indicated, the comments which follow are prompted principally by observation of undergraduate students. But they are probably influenced also by circumstances which are more likely to be found on the residential campus in a small town.

Student Power

The student body of an academic community wields power. This power may be circumscribed in various ways, and its exercise may be evident in indirect and subtle ways. It is still power, and power which cannot be eliminated or ignored by a faculty, by an administration, or by others.

Student power has at least three manifestations. One is economic. One is academic. The third is social. All three have an important impact upon the academic community. Interestingly enough, this power is seldom acknowledged, and it is at best but poorly structured. Student power is consequently often latent.

Indeed, it is probable that students themselves have little realization of the power which they do and can exercise. Many scholars and administrators take heart at this lack of understanding. An extremely militant student body can express its position in awesome and even dangerous proportions, as has been noted on occasion in universities of other countries.

In the United States, student interest tends to concentrate upon social rather than economic or academic power. The student is more apt to be excited by his emergence from home and parental supervision than by his status as a student. He is apt to be fairly docile in his attitude toward academic requirements. His response to his academic environment is individual and seldom organized. And it is this academic response in turn which has economic implications. It may be well to begin our review of student power with its economic manifestation.

The Economics of Student Behavior

Students are a major source of income to all colleges and universities, with only a few exceptions. In some of our best-known privately sponsored universities, universities of high academic reputation, student fees as a source of educational income are second only to federal government contracts and grants for research. In most privately sponsored liberal arts colleges, charges to students are the largest single source of educational income. In state-sponsored universities student fees are the second or third most important source of income in support of educational programs, coming after state tax support or federal government contracts and grants for research.

In the financing of the residence-hall program of a college or university, board and room charges usually constitute almost all of the available income to defray operating costs, including debt service. In such other auxiliary activities as a student health service and a student center, fees and charges paid by students are the principal source of revenue. In an artist and lecture program and even in intercollegiate athletics, a general fee paid by students is an important if not the preponderant source of income.

Thus when the total current operating income of a college or university is considered, including educational and general income, auxiliary service income, and student-aid income, fees and charges to students will almost always be found to be either the first or second source of income for most colleges and universities, whether they operate under public or private sponsorship. Students are a major economic asset. More than the academic enterprise would suffer if there were no students. The economic survival of most colleges and universities would be threatened if there were any substantial reduction in the number of students in our society. This simple fact tended to be overlooked by the manpower planners of World War II who wanted to mobilize all male youth for service in the armed forces.

The importance of student fees as a source of income to our colleges and universities raises far-reaching issues of social and economic policy. We can do no more here than sketch these. From the point of view of the social objectives of higher education, should students be expected to provide a major or preponderant source of income for our colleges and universities? To what extent should the social purposes of higher education be placed ahead of individual or personal goals in higher education? In some countries students are actually paid an income to attend higher education, but in those countries only a small proportion of youth are permitted to go to a college or university, and they are highly selected. In such countries higher education is largely if not entirely supported by government. In such countries social purposes are placed ahead of individual purposes, at least in the realm of higher education.

The economics of student charges as a source of income involves one of the peculiarities of a college or university as an economic unit. In general, expenditures in a college or university tend to increase proportionately with the size of the student body. There may be some economy of scale in a college or university, and within certain limits one or five or ten additional students represent a net increase of income without a corresponding increase of expenditure. The precise economic effects of larger enrollments upon levels of expenditure and the economic welfare of a college or university have not been established.

I am disposed to believe from limited evidence and experience that expansion of enrollment does bring with it certain important benefits in economic welfare for a college or university. I suspect that this among other factors explains why most colleges and universities in the United States have been willing to grow in enrollment size.

Here we are concerned primarily with the economic power exercised by students and how this power affects the general operation of a college or university. Obviously, by deciding to attend or not to attend a particular college or university, or by deciding to disenroll after initial attendance, students exert a definite economic impact upon the academic community. If large numbers of students were to decide to boycott a college or university, or to dissuade prospective students from enrolling, the income position of the college or university would suffer substantially. Two or three years of abstention could end the existence of a college or university.

Actually, the exercise of economic power in this consumer-preference fashion operates only occasionally in any given academic community. It has been said that the economic future of women's liberal arts colleges is threatened by a shift in consumer preference from the separate women's college to the coeducational college.[1] What effect this threat will actually have remains to be seen. In some instances, colleges and universities with a poor location in terms of transportation access or availability to nearby centers of population have perhaps suffered from limited enrollments, with correspondingly limited income. And some colleges and universities located in distressed economic areas often suffer economically because of an inability to charge student fees at the level needed to provide desired income.

Indeed, many administrators are fearful of raising student fees in any substantial amount at one time because they believe that students will shift to other colleges or universities. The elasticity of demand for a college education in relation to the level of charge for such education is one of the great eco-

[1] See Mabel Newcomer, *A Century of Higher Education for American Women* (New York: Harper & Brothers, 1959).

nomic unknowns of higher education. Only one careful study of this subject, to my knowledge, has ever been undertaken, and it concluded that the demand was more inelastic than popularly supposed.[2] Nonetheless, administrators of some privately sponsored colleges and universities have been critical of state-sponsored universities on the ground that they have not raised their fees enough, and that this prevents the private college or university from raising its charges to a needed level.

In any event, economic competition is one of the fears of administration in higher education. Even though these fears may be ill-founded, they nonetheless operate. Whether economic competition is desirable in higher education is a large subject. Furthermore, exactly what constitutes economic competition has never been too well defined. The relationship of price to quality is a factor seldom mentioned. Moreover, the noneconomic as against the economic motivations in college attendance have never been carefully explored. Finally, the colleges and universities with the highest charges to students tend at the same time to be those which spend the most money for student assistance. This practice of student aid certainly blunts the competitive economic status of various colleges and universities.

Moreover, as almost everyone interested in higher education knows today, colleges and universi-

[2] Richard H. Ostheimer, *Student Charges and Financing Higher Education* (New York: Columbia University Press, 1953).

ties have entered a seller's market. The demand for admission greatly exceeds the supply of college and university facilities for residence and instruction, especially in many of the best-known and most popular colleges and universities. The result is that many colleges and universities are little concerned about economic competition at the moment. The demand for their services is far greater than they can meet or than they are willing to meet. In a seller's market the consumer—in this instance the student—finds his economic power considerably lessened.

Within the academic community itself, student enrollment is again an expression of a form of economic power, or of consumer preference. Some professors are much more in demand than others. The reasons are not important to consider here. The popular professor is an economic asset to a college or university. The popular professor may attract students, and within the college or university he draws more students than many of his colleagues. The popular professor is a big income producer for the college or university he serves, and he may insist that he be compensated in terms of his economic production.

Most administrators in a college or university realize that the contribution or importance of a particular professor to the college or university cannot be measured by the income produced from high student enrollment. Student popularity may reflect other factors besides scholarly worth. And academic value may be contributed through other forms of scholarship than that indicated by large enrollments. Indeed, a Nobel laureate in physics may bring great distinction to a university, even though few students study with that particular scholar.

Perhaps another kind of economic power exercised by students should be mentioned, a kind of negative economic power. By their behavior at a particular college or university students can discourage or repel other forms of economic support. Students often forget this fact or tend to ignore it. Student income is not the exclusive source of income for a college or university, as we pointed out before. The individual college or university relies upon philanthropic and governmental income as well, and this is true whether a college or university is privately or publicly sponsored.

Large and small potential benefactors of a college or university may be alienated by what they consider the sloppy social patterns of student behavior. They may be alienated by stories of excessive liquor consumption or by the prevalence of many automobiles owned by students or their parents. They may be alienated by what they consider radical social ideas prevalent among students. There have even been potential benefactors who were alienated because they felt that students were too conservative in their social attitudes.

These considerations also influence legislators. Especially when there is popular dissatisfaction with levels of public spending and when there are many demands for increased public services, legislators ask questions and seek excuses to limit public expenditures for higher education. They may also desire to limit tax exemptions for higher education.

In other words, students can have some influence upon philanthropic and governmental support of higher education in the United States. When students do not pay the entire cost of the educational service they receive, they do not have the economic freedom to behave as they may please. There is a social obligation which goes along with social economic support of higher education.

In any event, students do exercise economic power in both a positive and negative sense. In their selection of one college or university as against another, students affect the economic well-being of particular colleges and universities. By their social behavior students may encourage or discourage philanthropic and governmental economic support of colleges and universities. The influence of the market place as well as the influence of philanthropy and government have their impact upon the economic welfare of the academic community.

Academic Power

Since 1900, higher education in the United States has experienced a steady increase in student enrollment. At the beginning of the twentieth century, enrollment numbered about 250,000 students. This represented an increase of nearly five times the number of students attending college in 1870. By 1910 the number of students was nearing 400,000; by 1920 it had risen to 600,000; by 1930 it was well over 1 million; by 1940 enrollment was over 1.5 million; by 1950 it had gone to 2.6 million, of which perhaps

800,000 were veterans; and by 1960 enrollment was over 3.6 million.[3]

Obviously, the enrollment growth of higher education represents in part an expansion of national population. But the major factor in enrollment growth has been the increasing proportion of young people of college age going to college. As of 1900, it has been estimated that 4 per cent of the college-age group were enrolled in college. As of 1950, if we exclude veterans whose higher education had been disrupted or postponed because of military service, about 20 per cent of the age group were enrolled in higher education. By 1960, with the veteran's "bulge" largely disappeared, enrollment in higher education represented over 35 per cent of the age group eighteen through twenty-one years. Actually, this last percentage in particular overstates the proportion of youth going to college, since it does not make allowance for the enrollment of graduate students and of other adults attending on a part-time basis, both of which categories of students have increased substantially in the past decade.

Nonetheless, it is evident that there has been an upward trend in the proportion of youth of college age enrolling in college during the twentieth century. Moreover, there are many who believe that this trend will continue until as many as 50 per cent of youth are pursuing some kind of formalized education beyond the high school. Whether all this education

[3] These figures are taken from reports of the Office of Education. They include part-time as well as full-time students, undergraduate and graduate, enrolled for credit.

should be called "higher" education is debatable. Indeed, I have serious doubts whether all of the 1960 enrollment should be so labeled, although it certainly constituted education beyond the high school level. The basic proposition remains that enrollment in higher education has grown greatly and that the increase has reflected both population growth and growth in the proportion of youth going to college.

These numbers have had a very real impact upon the academic programs of higher education. Indeed, there is a considerable debate whether changes in the curriculum of higher education have induced more students to enroll or whether more students have compelled colleges and universities to alter their programs. It seems likely, I believe, that both motivations for change have operated. It would be fruitless to try to decide which came first: the students and then curriculum change, or curriculum change and then larger and larger numbers of students.

Without doubt, a major change in the curriculum of higher education has taken place in this country; it began roughly in 1870 and continues down to this very day. Sometimes this change is attributed in good measure to the impact of the federal Morrill Act of 1862 and the consequent land grants to states for higher education to encourage instruction in, among other subjects, agriculture and the mechanic arts. In fact, there were critics within American colleges in the 1850s and 1860s who were advocating a curriculum more closely related to the realities of American life. The young nation had outgrown the rigorous classical curriculum imported from England, with its particular emphasis upon preparation for careers in theology and law. The result was a general and gradual change in which science, engineering, business administration, teacher education, and other professional applications of knowledge came to occupy an ever larger part of the college curriculum.[4]

The impact of increased undergraduate enrollment in our colleges and universities is sometimes demonstrated by reference to the types of bachelor's degrees now conferred. Today, between 20 and 25 per cent of strictly undergraduate degrees in the United States are conferred upon students who have prepared themselves for elementary and secondary schoolteaching. Another 16 per cent of all undergraduate degrees go to students of business administration. Nearly 10 per cent go to students of engineering, some 6 per cent to students of fine arts, 3 per cent to students of agriculture, and 3 per cent to students of home economics. Altogether these six fields of undergraduate interest account for better than 60 per cent of all undergraduate degrees conferred by American colleges and universities. The remaining 40 per cent of undergraduate degrees are distributed mostly among majors in the biological sciences, English, foreign languages, mathematics, the physical sciences, the social sciences, and philosophy and religion.

[4] These developments are recounted in Richard Hofstadter and C. DeWitt Hardy, *The Development and Scope of Higher Education in the United States* (New York: Columbia University Press, 1952); John S. Brubacher and Willis Rudy, *Higher Education in Transition* (New York: Harper & Brothers, 1958); and in other writings.

Nor have the universities with their varied undergraduate programs been alone in meeting the practical academic preferences of enlarged student bodies. The separate liberal arts college has broadened its scope of major fields of interest so that almost as many preprofessional or professional subjects are provided.[5] Indeed, the liberal arts colleges are accused of fostering a high degree of specialization upon their undergraduates who major in the disciplines, primarily as a result of the impact of graduate schools upon the colleges.[6]

The criticism that undergraduate education in the United States is excessively professional or specialized does not impress me particularly. A careful reading of the history of higher education in Western culture suggests that universities have always had professional objectives. Higher education has not claimed purely esoteric purposes of cultivating knowledge for its own sake. Higher education has been tied to practical goals. The classical curriculum of the British universities—primarily of Oxford and Cambridge—was a professional curriculum. The education provided was considered that most suitable for a gentle-

[5] See Earl J. McGrath and Charles H. Russell, *Are Liberal Arts Colleges Becoming Professional Schools?* (New York: Bureau of Publications, Teachers College, Columbia University, 1958).

[6] See Earl J. McGrath, *The Graduate School and the Decline of Liberal Education* (New York: Bureau of Publications, Teachers College, Columbia University, 1959). For a more balanced view of this issue see Bernard Berelson, *Graduate Education in the United States* (New York: McGraw-Hill Book Company, Inc., 1960).

man destined for a seat in Parliament or a place in the higher reaches of the civil service. Indeed, there is some question whether the classical curriculum was not continued in the United Kingdom beyond the time when it was relevant to the professional needs of British society.

In any event, American higher education realizes professional and specialized objectives, tempered by the degree of general education enforced by a particular college or university. These professional and specialized objectives serve the interests of American society, and these interests in turn are reflected by the academic preferences of undergraduate students.

Sometimes the concern is expressed that American higher education may be endeavoring to graduate more students than the professional demands of the society warrant.[7] Indeed, a government forecast from the Bureau of Labor Statistics in 1949 estimating that more engineers were being produced than could be employed is supposed to have discouraged students for several years from enrolling in engineering programs. In recent years government efforts have been devoted to encouraging more students to major in engineering science. In other fields as well, various manpower studies today suggest that, for the needs of our society, most professional fields will be undermanned during the next decade or two.

The academic power of American students is exerted in the interests of professional and specialized education. It is with some degree of student opposi-

[7] See Seymour E. Harris, *The Market for College Graduates* (Cambridge, Mass.: Harvard University Press, 1949).

tion that faculties are able to enforce requirements of general education. On occasion, for fear of competition from other colleges or universities, a faculty may refrain from imposing as rigorous requirements of general education as it might otherwise be willing to impose. We may well agree with President Keeney of Brown University when he says: "Students tend to forget that they have, in a way, 'hired themselves educated,' and that, having hired an institution, they are well advised to abide by the decisions of the institution." [8] It is not always a simple matter to persuade the student of the wisdom of this advice.

Student enrollment affects more than the scope and content of educational programs. It has great effect also upon the quality of these programs. Although higher education now enrolls on a full-time basis from 25 to 30 per cent of youth at eighteen years of age, this does not mean that our colleges and universities obtain the top 25 to 30 per cent of youth in terms of intellectual ability. On the contrary, the youth who enroll are spread out over the whole range of intellectual ability. To be sure, intellectual ability is not an easy characteristic to measure. Our customary standard of judgment is the rank of the high school graduate in his class in so far as grades are concerned, or his performance on a standardized test of college ability, or both.

By such criteria as we have of intellectual ability, we know that in the top 25 per cent of youth, one-fifth will not graduate from high school. Another two-

[8] Barnaby C. Keeney, "Decision-Making," *The Educational Record,* vol. 41 (July, 1960), p. 191.

fifths may not go on to college, for a variety of reasons from inadequate motivation to inadequate financial support.[9] Thus, only two-fifths of the top 25 per cent of all youth in terms of intellectual ability may enroll in college. Since the figures just quoted are ten years old, it seems probable that this record has improved somewhat. It may be that as many as three-fifths of the top-ability youth of our nation are now enrolling in colleges and universities. This still means, however, that perhaps an equal number of young people go to college who do not fall in the top 25 per cent of ability.

Even when we grant that ability cannot be clearly and unmistakably defined or identified, the fact remains that youth possessing a wide variety of ability find their way to college. It is also a fact that colleges and universities differ considerably in the quality of students whom they attract and retain. Certain colleges and universities are quite selective in their admission of students. Many state universities may open their doors wide but have a reputation for quality which results in a good deal of student self-selection. Other colleges and universities in order to operate must admit students whose ability levels are quite varied.

For the most part, students of high quality help to make a college or university of high quality. A few students of great ability may be found in almost any

[9] Byron S. Hollinshead, *Who Should Go to College?* (New York: Columbia University Press, 1952); and Dael Wolfle, *America's Resources of Specialized Talent* (New York: Harper & Brothers, 1954).

college or university. But without the presence of a goodly number of high-ability students a college or university cannot hope to achieve or maintain a reputation for academic excellence. Many colleges and universities are eager to attract good students. Although less well publicized than the rivalry for athletic talent, the rivalry among colleges and universities in the United States for high-ability students is vigorous and even bitter.

As the number of youth of college age expands in the United States, many colleges and universities hope to become increasingly selective in their admission of students. This hope is related to the objective of quality and is prompted by a desire to become a college or university of higher academic standard. In considerable degree, as the number of youth grows and as facilities remain limited, more and more colleges and universities will achieve a level of excellence not before attainable.

The point is that students by their selection of a particular college or university to attend have a definite impact upon the academic quality of that college or university. The faculty may desire an academic program of quality; the faculty may vote to establish such a program. But unless there is a response in terms of student ability and interest, the faculty desire is almost useless. Students have a considerable influence on academic quality.

On occasion at various colleges and universities student-government organizations have expressed a desire to participate in the formulation of academic

policy. In general, however, students know so little
about the component elements of academic policy that
they have little if anything to contribute to its discussion. A student body or a group of student leaders
willing to inform itself on such questions as general
education versus specialized education, the disciplines
versus the professions, undergraduate versus graduate
education, admission policy in relation to quality, the
academic calendar, systems of academic advising, curriculum construction, academic standards, and teaching methods could exercise a real influence upon
academic affairs in a college or university. For better
or worse, few undergraduate students will take the
time or make the effort to inform themselves on these
matters. In the absence of such careful preparation,
student participation in academic affairs is meaning-
less.[10]

Student power in the academic affairs of the
academic community is exerted primarily by the force
of numbers and the expression of individual preference in so far as enrollment in various programs of
various levels of quality is concerned. In these ways
students continue to influence academic performance
by a college or university.

[10] Professor David Riesman believes he observes some
signs that students are interested in these issues and can be
influential in their consideration within the academic community. See his article "Where Is the College Generation
Headed?" *The Atlantic,* vol. 204 (April, 1961), p. 39.

Social Power

In so far as students do organize themselves, their efforts are directed primarily into channels of social endeavor. Student housing becomes an element of social organization, whether it be centered in residence halls, clubs, or fraternities and sororities. From time to time some students, faculty members, and administrators have dreamed of making student housing a focal point of learning, through tutoring sessions, discussion groups, extensive libraries, and other devices. Usually these efforts have failed to realize their great goals, although some success has been achieved. Class organization, student senates and councils, interfraternity councils, dramatic and musical organizations, subject-matter clubs, publications, honorary societies—all these tend to promote social relations among students rather than extensive intellectual achievement by the individual.

American students appear to regard the social activity of college or university life—the second curriculum—as of great importance. There are many explanations why this situation exists. Indeed, one comforting thought is that student social behavior today is not too different from that which has existed throughout centuries. One is almost tempted to say that students have always been students, and that their behavior today falls into traditional patterns.

The social life of students in its most favorable light may be considered a kind of laboratory in which a practical education occurs simultaneously with the more abstract or theoretical education of the class-room. In this sense student social activity is a true second curriculum, providing valuable experience to students in many kinds of enterprise, from political campaigns to television production, from editing and publishing a newspaper to composing and producing a musical comedy, from classical drama to jazz concerts, from foreign language conversation to charitable money raising. Either students have much energy that the regular course of studies does not absorb, or students find the classroom insufficiently exciting to command their full-time allegiance. The social life of a college campus is learning through action.

Seeing undergraduate social life in a less favorable light, some commentators have suggested that it is only a slightly different and more expensive form of a general pattern of behavior evidenced by youth in our culture—a pattern which emphasizes irresponsibility, excitement, and pursuit of individual gratification. The argument runs that students on a college campus cannot be expected to behave differently from youth in our cities and elsewhere. If our culture, both youth and adult, tends to place value upon togetherness, other-direction, conformity, and the organization, then the student is not suddenly freed from this environmental influence. Rather, he seeks to reproduce in microcosm the larger world of which he has been an observer and in which he soon expects to be a participant.

Student social life is undoubtedly an important part of the maturation process. A good many years ago someone observed that it was unfortunate so important an activity as higher education had to coincide with emotionally so difficult a period of time in the life of youth. Perhaps the aspect of college life of which the undergraduate student is most aware is that college represents a break from the past. He has emerged from the shelter of his home. He has escaped from the confining attention and continual presence of parental love. He now associates on a plane of equality with a number of youth of his own age group and of some common interest. He has acquired a maximum of freedom with a minimum of responsibility.

The classroom may represent a good deal of frustration for the student. He may not have had a rigorous preparation for college studies at the secondary school level. He may be surprised by the indifference of the college teacher to whether he does his classroom work or not; the faculty member does not beg the student to study. The student does his assigned work or he fails and is dropped from college. The student is aware of competition in the classroom. With this new environment in which some succeed and some fail, certain students seek to achieve status among their peers by social leadership, from election to student offices to participation in less approved activities.

Perhaps above all else, the student is confronted with the necessity of finding some way to reconcile liquor and sex with his college studies. No matter how many regulations are written into the rule books, students will drink. It is considered a sign of maturity to possess and consume alcoholic beverages. It is a way to gain attention from fellow students while learning how to avoid the attention of college or university authorities and any other unhappy consequence. Similarly, the college student is much concerned about his personal relations with fellow students of the opposite sex. The male must have a girl, and the female must have a boy friend. This is a part of the college expectation.

To liquor and sex is added the further complication of the automobile. Some colleges and universities still endeavor to prevent students from having automobiles. They hold to the belief that cars are an undesirable expense and a definite interference with academic study. Some colleges and universities have surrendered any attempt to control the possession of automobiles and simply struggle to provide enough parking places. Other colleges and universities have sought a compromise, such as banning automobiles for freshmen and sophomores but permitting them for juniors and seniors. However a college or university decides to meet the problem, the difficulty is never resolved. The automobile, so vital to the culture and economy of America, is at best a nuisance and at worst an outright obstacle to higher education.

This background of understanding is important to a discussion of student government. On most college and university campuses, the faculty and administration have delegated considerable power of self-government to students. Within certain limits students may form various organizations for social purposes. They may publish a newspaper, a yearbook, a literary magazine, and sometimes a so-called "humorous" magazine (that bane of an administrator's life, as I found out as a student and as an administrator). They may produce musical shows. They may organize dances, carnivals, sport shows, songfests, intramural athletic contests, and other endeavors. Over all this activity sits, in some kind of general oversight, a student council or senate.

What are the issues which rock student government from time to time? Are they issues of academic excellence, academic freedom, academic financing? No. They are almost always social, and sooner or later they involve the three basic issues of liquor, sex, and automobiles. Seldom if ever are students interested in more stringent rules against drinking. Rather they want the rules or their enforcement relaxed. Seldom if ever are students interested in cutting down the number of dances and parties, in regulating more strictly the visiting arrangements for men and women students, or in reducing the public display of affection. Rather, student government wants later visiting hours and fewer restrictions upon the conduct of men and women. Seldom if ever are students interested in eliminating automobiles from the campus. Rather they want more cars.

Student government is thus almost always in conflict with faculty members and administrative officials about the social life of a campus. Students argue that they should be treated as adults, even if they don't want to behave like adults. Students claim they cannot behave like responsible citizens if they are not trusted to be such. Students resent interference with freedom, which too often is confused with license. Some faculty members and administrators sympathize with such points of view and even encourage students to express them. Others point to the need for social restraint during college years until students accept the full responsibilities of profession, family, and community. The argument has been going on for a long time and will no doubt continue for a still longer time.

To some adults an open and frank acknowledgment of student social difficulties is grounds for restricting the opportunity for higher education. If liquor, sex, and automobiles are so important to students, why should society make such strenuous efforts through philanthropic giving and taxation to support colleges and universities? Such an attitude overlooks two or three essential facts. In our culture, liquor, sex, and automobiles are a problem of all youth, not just of college students. Secondly, these problems exist in the adult population as well. These are human problems; the liquor and sex problems have bothered many a culture as long as there has been a recorded history. A college or university campus simply concentrates a goodly number of young people in a relatively confined area and focuses public attention upon their behavior.

Many colleges or universities acquire a general reputation among students and parents based upon the prevailing social attitudes and practices of the student body. A particular campus may be "highly social," meaning that there are many dances, parties, and other social events. A particular student body may be made up of "heavy drinkers." Another campus is

known as very strict in its social regulations. Sometimes these are evaded by wholesale transfer of social
activity to another campus or to nearby large cities
every weekend. Some campuses are known as "liberal" in their social attitudes, believing that a student's social life is his own business so long as he
meets exacting academic standards. Other campuses
endeavor to guide students into a satisfactory mixing
of academic and social activity.

Sometimes social attitudes become confused with
intellectual attitudes. On some campuses social nonconformity becomes the great conformity; the student
in the process of exploring the world of ideas must
cast aside respect for or conformity to prevailing social
customs as a means of proclaiming his intellectual
freedom. For a student to admit that he believes in
chaperonage of young men and women is like admit-
ting to a belief in phlogiston or necromancy. Social
customs are superstitions to be discarded as one learns
the real "facts" of the world. One can only be amused
by these attitudes, and ask questions about the exact
relationship between knowledge and social custom,
and recall that the youth who make the most noise
about nonconformity often end up years later being
strong conformists to social custom.

Nonetheless, student attitudes about social life
on a college campus are not readily changed. Once a
set of rules or attitudes becomes widely accepted by
one or more student generations, it becomes an accepted code of conduct. Any effort at change which
might be interpreted as restricting previous student
freedom will be vigorously resisted. It is not easy to

experiment on a college campus with social regulations. Once a change is made, even on a temporary basis, any abandonment of the experiment will usually be opposed.

Finally, a word should be mentioned about student participation in disciplinary activity on a campus. Many times boards or committees are established to decide the guilt or innocence of an individual student charged with violation of a rule. Sometimes these "courts" are composed entirely of students. Sometimes they are composed jointly of students and faculty members. In this way students participate in the determination of infractions of rules and in the imposition of penalties. My own observation is that most students elected or assigned to disciplinary boards take their duties quite seriously.

The College Environment

The college student sees his campus through his own eyes. Whether his image coincides with that of faculty, alumni, and administration is uncertain. Whether his view is less realistic is debatable. The fact is that the student has his particular belief about the characteristics of the college he attends, and this attitude does much to create a college or university which fits the conception.

Professor Robert Pace of Syracuse has made a special study of the beliefs students hold about the college they attend.[11] Pace constructed a College Char-

[11] See C. Robert Pace, "'Five College Environments," *College Board Review,* vol. 41 (Spring, 1960), p. 24.

acteristics Index consisting of 300 statements about college life. The statements referred to curriculum, instructional practices, academic policies, social rules and regulations, student organizations, social activities, and campus features. This index was administered to students at different colleges and universities in the United States. The students were asked to say whether they thought any given statement was true or false as applied to the individual college or university they attended.

From this study Professor Pace has identified five major types of environment as perceived by students themselves. These five types have differences among themselves in either intellectual or social terms. The first type of college environment is preponderantly humanistic, reflective, and sentient. Students are given special opportunities to consider and discuss important works in music, art, and drama. Concerts, lectures, and art exhibits draw large crowds. Class discussions are vigorous and intense. Students set high standards of achievement and place their intellectual endeavors above social activities. The second type of environment is much the same as the first, except that here the intellectual emphasis is upon science and upon competition for achievement. Academic survival is left to the individual. Students come from a wide variety of national, religious, and social backgrounds. Student organizations are not closely supervised. Students are eager to make their mark in their chosen field of science or engineering. In both types of environment there is a high degree of individualism and some tendency toward social nonconformity.

The third type of environment is one where the practical and the applied are emphasized rather than the abstract and theoretical. Students are concerned to establish their status with their peers and tend to accept their status in relation to authority. Students are interested in professional fields of study. There is little student interest in criticizing teaching methods or social regulations. Student campaigns for elective office are intense. There is a recognized group of student leaders. There are many social activities. The fourth type of college environment is one with special emphasis on friendliness. Faculty and students must get to know each other. Service to community is one of the principal objectives of the college. Counseling and guidance are extensive. Student helpfulness one to another is expected. Courses of study are clearly laid out, and social activities are carefully planned.

In the fifth environment, social nonconformity is rampant. Students are noisy and inattentive at lectures and concerts. Others are expected to adapt to the student, not the student to others. There are occasional plots for some kind of escapade or rebellion. Student activities are informal and largely unplanned. Students are interested in their course work in a kind of vague way, without too much concern whether they complete particular programs or projects. The students are in conflict with the idea of an other-directed community.

At best such a classification scheme presents generalizations which will not necessarily apply perfectly to any one college or university or to all students of a single college or university. There may be gradations of difference within any major category. Nonetheless, the types identified by Professor Pace will be immediately recognizable to one who has visited a number of college campuses.

Certainly it would be very difficult for the faculty or administration of a college or university to set out specifically to change its environmental type without a great deal of cooperation from students. Moreover, student characteristics would have purposefully to be altered through admission practices over the span of several years. Once a college or university falls into a type-pattern, it is not likely to change substantially, except over a considerable period of time.

It may be mentioned here that there has been a great deal of discussion in recent years about whether a college education has any major impact upon the value judgments of students. Professor Philip E. Jacob of the University of Pennsylvania reached the conclusion that the values of American students are remarkably homogeneous. Students tend to be contented in regard to their day-to-day activity and their future outlook. They are self-centered. They have an easy tolerance of differences among themselves. They profess traditional moral values. They acknowledge a need for religion. They are dutifully responsive toward government without a feeling of obligation for the public welfare. They expect and fear war, but are generally indifferent to international affairs. They are convinced of the good of college in general and of their own college or university in particular. This general array of values the college student tends to bring to college with him, and he is likely to depart with the same values intact. The major impact of college is to reinforce or socialize these values, not to alter them. There is little evidence that a particular form of curriculum or a particular type of instructor makes any important difference in these values.[12]

These findings by Professor Jacob have been much discussed and criticized.[13] The then vice president of the University of New Hampshire has presented one of the major counterarguments.[14] Dr. Eddy began a study at twenty colleges and universities with three assumptions: that American colleges are consciously concerned about the character of students, that it is not desirable to separate the education of the intellect from values which impinge upon the thought and life of a student, and that colleges can and do modify the value judgments of students.

First of all, Dr. Eddy found that the "level of expectancy" in student achievement and student attitudes had much to do with what happens to a student in college. For the most part this level of expectancy rested with members of the faculty, but students likewise could influence the intellectual demands made upon them. Secondly, Dr. Eddy declared that a college could not hope to have any impact upon the

[12] Philip E. Jacob, *Changing Values in College* (New York: Harper & Brothers, 1957).

[13] I find on my shelves seven booklets, pamphlets, or journals published after 1957 criticizing or modifying these findings.

[14] Edward D. Eddy, Jr., *The College Influence on Student Character* (Washington, D.C.: American Council on Education, 1959).

development of a student's character unless special attention was given to a concept of teaching. Students seemed to respect teachers who had a commitment to certain values, made these clear, but did not try to win any converts. Students were suspicious of or confused by the faculty member who claimed objectivity about competing values. Students wanted to know why a faculty member had embraced a certain set of values and wanted to understand that these values came from reasoning, not merely from personal prejudices. In the third place, Dr. Eddy emphasized the importance of winning student interest from the very beginning of the freshman year in a program of study and in individual courses. If the student sees little relevance between what he learns and what he will become, his behavior and attitudes as a student seem unimportant.

Dr. Eddy considered with some care the role students might assume in planning a curriculum and in controlling their social activity. He was disposed to believe that students might well take more responsibility for both and that they might develop a system of values from action as well as from study. But he acknowledged that situations might vary from campus to campus. In this connection, it would have been helpful if he had had the benefit of Professor Pace's findings about the student image of the academic and social environment. In so far as religion itself was concerned, Dr. Eddy concluded that students were neither committed nor hostile; they were interested in religion but were questioning what it might mean and what it might require. Finally, Dr. Eddy declared: "The essential purpose of the college is training for intelligent behavior." [15] This, he insisted, means more than the acquisition of knowledge; it includes the ability "to make relevant judgments and wise choices guided by the discipline of logical method." The educated person is one with attitudes, habits, and allegiances influenced or conditioned by the experience of higher education.

One may argue at length—as many students, faculty members, and administrators have—about the objectives and the methods of higher education in leading students to question or reinforce value judgments. On at least one aspect of the subject, there appears to be some agreement. The student does not come to college with a blank slate on which the college writes a system of values—or as the British sociologist Hobhouse defined them, "standards held with conviction." The college student comes from a culture in which his family and school life have tended to make him the center of attention, in which he has usually had much encouragement and few frustrations. This may not be true of youth who come from that 15 per cent of the families constituting the lower lower class of American society, but few college students are recruited from this class. In college the student faces a more challenging and a more competitive environment than any he has yet encountered. It is an environment in which he must meet the academic challenge of his teachers and the social challenge of

[15] *Ibid.*, p. 168.

his peers. The reaction depends upon an interaction of student and environment. The student himself has much to do with the result.

Conclusion

Students make a difference in the academic community. Their ability, their motivation, their interests, their attitudes, and their standards held with conviction—all these have their impact upon the academic and social life in any college or university.

In so far as academic interests are concerned, it is my personal observation that students tend to fall in one of three categories. There are some who enroll in college because they haven't anything else to do; they want to get away from home, they want to be near a boy or girl friend, they are not ready to go to work or assume family responsibilities. These students usually fall by the wayside before four years are ended, although some will expend sufficient energy to remain and graduate. Then there are those students with an immediate, practical interest. They want to become a schoolteacher, an accountant, a doctor, a lawyer, an engineer, an architect, a commerial artist, a journalist, a market analyst, a physicist. These students want courses which fit their goal. They are not interested in ideas as such; they are interested in a specific field of knowledge as a tool. They are willing to expend the effort to meet their objective, but little beyond that. They want everything they study to be relevant to their present purpose. Thirdly, there are students highly motivated toward abstract ideas, either in the humanities and social sciences or in the biological and physical sciences. They are eager to consider and discuss various theories in their general field of interest. Knowledge is to them a great excitement.

A relatively small college or institute may have a homogeneous student body of one kind of student, especially the third kind. A large state, municipal, or private university of varied programs will have all three kinds of students. These varied arrangements do much to determine the academic atmosphere of the college or university.

In so far as social life is concerned, students tend, I believe, to fall in one of two categories. There are those interested in an active social life along lines of traditional or cultural conformity. Then there are those who want to assert independence of the general culture. They may as alumni be absorbed by that culture and indeed become its staunch adherents. For a time they want at least the illusion of nonconformity, and the college years provide the opportunity. Here again these varied attitudes affect the academic environment.

Student social organization and student government could be a more effective force in the academic community if social objectives were more clearly defined by students themselves, and if students revealed more readily some evidence of responsible self-control in such matters as liquor, sex, and automobiles. Because students are students, these "ifs" set almost impossible standards of desired behavior. Nonetheless, students do mature as undergraduates; they do grow intellectually and socially.

By the self-selection of their interests and of the college or university most likely to meet them, students are a vital element of power in the academic community.

Chapter 5

Alumni

ALUMNI OF A COLLEGE or university are more than the educational product of higher learning. They are also participants in the power structure of the academic community. Indirectly and directly, alumni exercise a real influence upon the behavior of higher education. It is an influence which has both its praiseworthy and questionable aspects.

Like so many other features of American life, college alumni have their caricature or stereotype. There is supposed to be a typical alumnus, and he is usually pictured as a successful business or professional man who still lives the student pranks and the athletic prowess of his own day, who believes that the present-day student doesn't measure up to his own contemporaries, who wants the college or university to remain the way it was "in the good old days," and who expects alma mater to win every football game. This typical alumnus is not so much interested in the intellectual progress of higher education as in its outward evidence of material progress: new buildings,

149

well-kept lawns, new recreational fields. When he is concerned about what the student learns, this alumnus is alarmed that the faculty is made up of "subversives, collectivists, atheists, and do-gooders."

Interestingly enough, the common portrait of an alumnus is always that of a man. The alumna seldom is pictured as having any identifiable character at all. On occasion one finds the statement that the woman college graduate struggles through life caught between the demands of family and the potentiality of intellectual or professional achievement. Only a few women are thought able to attain success in both fields of endeavor. Except for examination of this inherent frustration, the alumnae of higher education receive little attention.

As I have suggested, the typical portrait of the college alumnus is a stereotype. It is an impression perhaps induced by the noisy demand for attention which comes from some alumni. It is far from a realistic representation. College and university alumni, like many other identifiable groups, are not of any one kind. Alumni comprise several million people, and they have many different likes and dislikes, many different achievements and failures, many different hopes and fears. There is no such thing as a typical alumnus.

There is perhaps one common characteristic of most alumni. They tend to maintain some interest throughout life in the particular college or university where they obtained their higher education. I shall have more to say about this loyalty in a moment. Needless to observe, not all alumni experience this sense of allegiance to the same degree or in the same way. There are even those who develop a considerable hostility to their college or university, an attitude which sometimes reflects disappointment in one's personal career. What is surprising is not that this hostility should occasionally occur as that it should be so rare among alumni.

In a formal and direct sense, alumni of a college or university exercise some influence in the academic community through the board of trustees. In the United States there are two customary methods for the selection of trustees for colleges and universities. In general, the boards of privately sponsored colleges and universities are self-perpetuating, the board electing new members as former members resign, retire, or die. Sometimes in church-related colleges and universities the trustees are formally chosen by a church body. For the publicly sponsored colleges and universities, boards of trustees or of regents tend to be appointed for a fixed term of years by the governor of the state, often subject to confirmation by the state senate. In a few instances, trustees or regents are popularly elected, and in at least one case they are selected by the state legislature meeting in joint session.

In various ways these general practices have been altered to recognize alumni representation. At Harvard University, the official corporation is made up of seven persons known as the President and Fellows, who are self-perpetuating. On the other hand, many of the acts of the President and Fellows must be approved by a Board of Overseers of 30 members, 5 of whom are elected each year for six-year terms by the alumni. This dual arrangement, however, is to be found in only one or two other colleges or universities. At the Massachusetts Institute of Technology, there are 58 members of the board, 15 of whom are nominated by the alumni association and are then automatically elected trustees. Of 24 trustees at Columbia University, 6 are nominated by the alumni. Of 34 board members at the Johns Hopkins University, 6 are nominated by the alumni association. Of 49 trustees at Cornell University, 10 are elected by the alumni. Similar provisions exist in other colleges and universities. Ordinarily, certain trustees are elected by the alumni association, usually for a stated term of office. The number is usually a minority of the total membership. Yet in practice, boards may of course elect to membership individuals who happen to be alumni of the college or university.

Among publicly sponsored universities, there are certain instances where alumni have some voice in the selection of trustees. Thus at Pennsylvania State University, 9 of 32 board members are elected by the alumni body. At Indiana University, 3 of 8 members are elected by the alumni. At Purdue University, on the other hand, all 9 board members are appointed by the governor, but 3 of these are nominated by the alumni association. At the University of Kentucky, the law provides that of the 15 trustees, the governor must appoint 3 who are alumni. At the University of Arkansas, 6 of the 10 trustees appointed by the governor must be alumni. Yet, in Iowa where there is a single state board of regents for two universities and one college, the governor may not appoint more than 1 out of 9 regents from the alumni body of any one of the three schools. Obviously, the lawmakers in Iowa feared alumni would be prejudiced in favor of one university or college if too many served on the joint board.

In practice it seems likely that governors tend to appoint alumni as trustees of state-sponsored universities, regardless of legal provisions. Governors can expect alumni as trustees to give a good deal of attention to the university and to know something about its affairs.

Regardless then of the formal requirements of charters or state statutes, alumni tend to have a prominent place among the trustees of a college or university. This is a natural development, reflecting the interest in and support of college or university activities by alumni. Nonetheless, as trustees, alumni serve in an individual capacity and express their own personal judgment on the issues coming before the board. Trustees do not serve as representatives of the alumni body, no matter how they may be selected or how influential they may have been in alumni affairs.

The alumni body as a whole or as a dues-paying association exercises a direct influence in college or university affairs to the extent that it has a voice in the actual nomination or election of members of the board of trustees. These trustees may be reelected, or other alumni may be elected to serve on a rotating basis. Except in the election or nomination of trustees, an alumni organization does not usually have any direct voice in the decision-making process of a

college or university. It may have meetings and pass
resolutions. These are not necessarily binding upon
the trustees or other elements of the academic community.

Indirectly, an alumni organization may have a
good deal of influence in college or university affairs.
In part, this influence arises from the role of an
alumni association in raising an annual fund for the
support of a college or university. These annual funds
are so important in many instances that administrators—and faculty and students as well—must necessarily be sensitive to alumni interests in the operation
of the college or university. In part, this influence
arises from the role of an alumni association in con-
sidering the academic and other activities of a college
or university. Sometimes the alumni association sets
up visiting committees which spend a day or two a
year meeting with the faculty of a department, a college or school of a university, or other academic unit.
Such meetings give faculty members an opportunity
directly to acquaint alumni with their problems—
problems which too often involve building facilities
or expenditure levels. Yet alumni may get a better
impression of monetary requirements from these visits
than they get from listening to statements by the president or from reading college or university appeals for
support.

Indirectly, through fund raising, through formal
or informal visitation, through active interest in college affairs, alumni exercise some influence upon the
academic community. Just how great or extensive this
influence may be, it is impossible to say. Alumni

power, like power in the academic community generally, is seldom if ever pushed to extreme. Alumni power is a mysterious reality which exists but is usually not aroused.

A few years ago a young graduate of Yale University put forth the proposition that the faculty of the university was morally and constitutionally responsible to the trustees of Yale, and that the trustees in turn were responsible to the alumni.[1] He went on to assert that the faculty was accordingly bound to transmit to students the wisdom, insight, and value judgments which in the opinion of the trustees would enable the students as citizens to make the optimum adjustment to their community, their nation, and their world. He added that he believed the trustees to be committed to belief in God and the current economic system. These beliefs should therefore be incorporated in all academic teaching.

Mr. Buckley declared: "The responsibility to govern Yale falls ultimately on the shoulders of her alumni." [2] He did not explain how this responsibility should be structured. Presumably, the alumni body— he did not indicate whether this meant all alumni or only those belonging to the alumni association— would elect the members of the board of trustees. These trustees would then apparently be expected to represent the alumni, and by a system of reelection the trustees would discover whether they had in fact

[1] William F. Buckley, Jr., *God and Man at Yale: The Superstitions of Academic Freedom* (Chicago: Henry Regnery Company, 1951).
[2] *Ibid.*, p. 194.

represented a majority of the alumni successfully. The trustees in turn would in some way supervise and direct the content of instruction provided by the faculty.

In his introduction to the volume, Mr. John Chamberlain argued that for the faculty of a university alone to control the aims of education would, "pursued to its logical conclusion," establish an "elite of professorial untouchables." Such an elite would be able to perpetuate itself as it saw fit. Mr. Chamberlain added: "This is caste rule as applied to education; it might be unkind to call it 'Fascism,' but it is certainly not democracy."

Mr. Chamberlain did not ask whether the profession of scholarship was essentially different in power and responsibility from such professions as law, medicine, or theology. Nor did he suggest exactly how the profession of scholarship should be responsibly controlled, unless we are to conclude that he endorsed the hierarchical system proposed by Mr. Buckley.

It is not relevant to our concern here to examine the substance of Mr. Buckley's specific criticisms of the Yale faculty: that the faculty was not objective or impartial in its attitude toward the great value issues of our day. As to Christianity versus agnosticism or atheism, Mr. Buckley insisted that the Yale faculty was preponderantly agnostic or atheistic. As to individualism versus collectivism in the economic system, Mr. Buckley argued that the faculty was preponderantly collectivistic in point of view, and he seemed to argue that collectivism and communism were about the same thing.[3] These interpretations of faculty point of view at Yale may or may not be accurate.

Our interest here is in the idea of trustee responsibility to the alumni body and of faculty responsibility indirectly to the alumni body. This proposal certainly represents a new conception of responsibility in the academic community, and it is certainly contrary to the conception of structure in the academic community set forth in this volume. Our interpretation here of the academic community is intended to represent current reality.

The proposal that alumni should elect all trustees of a privately sponsored university—and perhaps that the voters should elect all trustees of a state-sponsored university—does not correspond with prevailing practice. Furthermore, the proposal that faculty should teach according to instructions from these trustees does not correspond with present practice. As I have suggested, I believe the prevailing conception is that faculty members have a professional responsibility as individuals and as a company of scholars to determine the instructional curriculum and the course content provided by a college or university.

To propose a different system of responsibility is to suggest that faculty members are not professionally responsible individuals but that they are employees of the trustees, expected faithfully to carry out the instructional directives of the trustees. To propose a hierarchical system of authority for a college or university is to suggest that trustees, and alumni who elect trustees, are competent to determine what shall

[3] *Ibid.*, p. 46.

be taught in the classroom and that trustees can transmit such instructional directives effectively.

Any such system of hierarchical authority assumes that the essence of democracy in higher education must be realized through a system of elections. Individuals cannot exercise a personal professional responsibility, and trustees cannot exercise in their realm of competence a collective sense of moral responsibility. I find it impossible to accept this conception of desirable organizational structure. I believe democracy is served by individual moral sense as well as by the moral sense of trustees. Nor am I unmindful of the many political thinkers who have feared the tyranny of a majority.

At the same time, it must be made clear that alumni are not without power in the academic community. Alumni do elect in many instances a part of the membership of a board of trustees. Individually, and in groups, alumni may criticize their college or university for various alleged failures or faults, even as did Mr. Buckley. These criticisms may influence the behavior of the academic community in various ways. Such criticism is not likely to be ignored unless it appears to be completely unreasonable or entirely a matter of personal prejudice.

Colleges and universities depend in considerable degree upon the assistance and support of alumni. They cannot afford to ignore the existence of the alumni or their varied points of view. As much as is possible, therefore, the academic community endeavors to accommodate their desires and suggestions.

The Role of Alumni as College Graduates

The power of alumni to influence the academic community depends in large part upon the knowledge and interest the alumni have in higher education. Yet the simple fact of the situation is that few alumni have learned very much about higher education as a social institution, about the objectives and operations of higher education, or about the organization and financing of our colleges and universities.

Alumni are a major product of higher education. Yet alumni know little about the process of education except that part of it which they as individuals have experienced, and they know little about colleges and universities except the one they personally attended. There is a general disposition among alumni to accept higher education as a good and to want a similar opportunity for their children, but this attitude is an act of faith rather than an expression of factual knowledge and careful reasoning.

It is ironic indeed that the college and university alumnus, the individual in society who has directly benefited from the work of higher education, should know so little about the institution in which he has been a participant. The alumnus is a graduate in a particular field of learning. If his college was a small one, he has probably developed a considerable sense of identity with the college as a whole. If his undergraduate or professional education was obtained in a large university, he is aware of the part in which he enrolled but probably little concerned with the remainder. The alumnus tends to take higher education for granted.

How many college graduates have any idea of the number of undergraduate bachelor's degrees conferred the year of their graduation throughout the United States? Today the number of college students receiving a degree for four years of college study is somewhere around 14 per cent of the age group. For every graduate, there are at least six other persons today who have not completed a college education. As of 1960, it appeared that about 7 or 8 per cent of the adult population of the United States were college graduates. The alumnus is therefore a substantial minority element in our nation. It is estimated that by 1980 only 10 per cent of the adult population will have college degrees. It might be thought that college alumni would have a sense of identity by the mere fact of their limited number.

Yet college graduates are widely scattered throughout the various sections of the United States, and in their communities and their professional lives they are closely associated with many persons who are not college graduates. The equalitarian tradition is so strong in American society that many alumni avoid any indication of snobbishness based upon college graduation. Moreover, in the business development of American society up until just recent time, achievement was often the result of individual shrewdness, ability, and good fortune rather than of education. For these and other reasons, the college graduate has not been a cohesive element in the structure and op-

eration of society. This situation may perhaps be in
process of change.

If the college graduate does not appear to have
a particular sense of social identity in the United
States, he seems to have even less awareness of the
purposes and the social role of higher education. Let
us take as an illustration the basic problem confronting higher education which has been so well discussed
by John W. Gardner of the Carnegie Corporation.[4]
In an open society—that is, one in which there is no
hereditary social stratification—individual differences
in ability and energy may be left to fix each person's
place. This is a society of competitive performance,
and in its extreme form it is likely to result in the
impoverishment of some and in an extreme concentration of wealth in the hands of a few. This in turn
is very apt in a short time to become again an hereditary social structure. An open society, in order to remain open, must curb the extremes of competitive
performance and provide some protection for the less
able, the less energetic, the less aggressive. These persons may be the parents of youngsters who are more
able than they, just as persons of great achievement
may have offspring of lesser ability.

While emphasizing individual achievement in
the open society of the United States, we have at the
same time endeavored to keep competitive performance within certain limits. Perhaps no single social
force is so important in promoting individual achievement today as higher education. But along with this

[4] John W. Gardner, *Excellence: Can We Be Equal and
Excellent Too?* (New York: Harper & Brothers, 1961).

social importance which we attribute to higher education, we also tend to promote equalitarianism by permitting access to higher education to large numbers of youth, and in addition we sometimes tend to lower the quality standards of higher education required for graduation. Moreover, in our financial support of higher education, we promote equality of opportunity by providing some support to potential students of good academic promise but limited economic resources.

This mutual accommodation of competitive performance and equalitarianism is a continuing problem for American society. It is equally a continuing problem for American higher education. The dimensions of the problem have become even greater because of the world situation in which our nation now finds itself. We must promote excellence in higher education not simply because of a concern with individual competitive performance but even more because of a concern with our national competitive performance. Higher education has greater purpose to achieve than ever before.

We are not concerned here, however, to discuss this perplexing problem of higher education: how to promote excellence while remaining sympathetic to the need for later restraints on individual performance in the interests of the equalitarian traditions of our society and in the interests of our commitment to an open society. We refer to this problem, perhaps the most important single problem facing higher education, simply to illustrate our particular issue here. How many college alumni in America are discussing this problem, analyzing its importance in terms of national objectives, and exploring its dimensions? How many alumni meetings are devoted to consideration of this subject? How many alumni publications are continually bringing this concern to the attention of alumni?

Yet if alumni are going to have a major impact upon the functioning of the academic community, this is the very kind of problem which they must be studying and about which they must have some definite, reasonable point of view to advance.

I would like to mention still another illustration which bears both upon the problem of excellence just outlined and upon the role of alumni as college graduates. Frank H. Bowles of the College Entrance Examination Board divides the some 1,800 colleges and universities in the country into three categories in terms of admission standards.[5] These three categories he terms: (1) preferred, (2) standard, and (3) easy. Mr. Bowles asserts that at present there are about 150 colleges and universities in the preferred category with considerable prestige and highly selective standards of admission. About 800 colleges and universities, according to Mr. Bowles, belong to the standard category, where admission is only slightly selective but where students of obviously low college ability or motivation are discouraged from attendance. In the third place, there are another 800 colleges and univer-

[5] I am using an article by Mr. Bowles entitled "Who Gets Into College?" which was prepared for Editorial Projects for Education, Inc., and reproduced widely in counseling publications and college magazines in 1961.

sities, especially junior colleges, where admission requirements are practically nonexistent. Any high school graduate is eligible for enrollment in these colleges and universities.

Mr. Bowles is discussing only admission standards. He says nothing about retention standards. In practice, some colleges and universities labeled "standard" in terms of admission requirements may have retention requirements which are as high as those of the "preferred" colleges and universities. Mr. Bowles does acknowledge that colleges and universities may change their status, and actually suggests that some of those in the standard classification may be in process of moving into the preferred category, and some of those in the easy classification may be moving into the standard category.

It is not important here whether we would be disposed to agree with Mr. Bowles in his system of classification or his quantitative estimates. What is important is the fact of differences among colleges and universities in their standards both of admission and retention of students. These differences do exist. And as Mr. Bowles indicates, the category in which a particular college or university falls may change over a period of time. The reasons for these differences and for changes in status are of vital concern to the United States in terms of what society as a whole and families as units expect of higher education. Yet here again one is compelled to ask: What are college alumni as a group doing to inform themselves about this problem and to express a point of view concerning it?

There is a vast array of problems confronting higher education in the United States.[6] These problems range from objectives and purposes to curricular requirements and financial support. They are not subject to simple solution. There are competing values involved in almost every single issue. And by its very nature the academic community tends fortunately to avoid extremes. Yet the problems cannot be ignored, and in various ways we must learn to live with them and to ameliorate their most mischievous consequences.

Alumni as college graduates should above all other elements in society at large have a sympathetic understanding of these problems. As a group, alumni should be working toward the adjustment of these problems. If college alumni are not concerned, who else can we expect to take an interest?

I do not wish to suggest that alumni are not interested in the various issues confronting higher education, but I do imply that college alumni as a group are not so well informed and so concerned about these problems as might be expected or desired. Many alumni as individuals do give a great deal of time to the problems of the particular college or university of which they are graduates. Perhaps this is all that reasonably may be asked. Perhaps this is enough.

College graduates lead active lives in their professions, their business enterprise, and their communities. They have little time to give to some vague

[6] These are well summarized in Algo D. Henderson, *Policies and Practices in Higher Education* (New York: Harper & Brothers, 1960).

social agency known as higher education. They are aware that great changes are in process. They are more aware that the fate of their own sons and daughters may be at stake, but this interest becomes personal rather than social. As community, business, and professional leaders, they are eager to know what is happening, but seldom does this generalized concern carry over into community or other action.

To some extent the absence of an understanding about higher education in general among college alumni may be traced back to student days. As students, few graduates learned anything specific or detailed about higher education itself. Faculty members seldom discuss problems of higher education. Even where higher education as a social problem is relevant to a particular field of knowledge, such as sociology, economics, or government, it is more often ignored than considered.[7] If the student does not become acquainted with higher education as an institution, the alumnus must begin to learn for himself. Sometimes he never begins.

The answer to this failure on the college campus is most certainly *not* a course in higher education for all undergraduates. Rather, if alumni are to be better informed about higher education, all faculty members

[7] I offer in evidence a volume edited by Jack W. Peltason and James M. Burns, *Functions and Policies of American Government* (Englewood Cliffs, N.J.: Prentice-Hall, Inc., 1958) which considers fiscal and monetary policy, foreign policy, military policy, transportation, agriculture and natural resources, government and business, government and labor, public health and welfare, public housing, and civil rights but has not a word to say about education!

must likewise be better informed and more willing to take time to discuss higher education objectively, fairly, and comprehensively, and not just in terms of the personal frustrations or bitterness of the individual faculty member in his own environment. The college graduate might have an extensive role to play in American society in consideration of and decision making about higher education. There is little evidence to support any proposition that this role at present is extensive or particularly influential.

College or University Loyalty

If college alumni as a social group exercise little influence upon higher education as an institution, their impact upon particular colleges and universities is much more evident. In large part, colleges and universities depend upon their alumni to maintain a continuing, direct interest in their individual well-being. And in large part, alumni tend to evidence a considerable loyalty to the particular college or university where they graduated.

It is difficult to identify the various ingredients of this loyalty. Some have pictured it as centering primarily in intercollegiate athletics. As I have suggested, this is more a caricature than a portrait. Alumni do manifest a good deal of interest in the athletic fortunes of their college or university. This is something tangible, something which requires little drain upon one's mental abilities, and something entertaining. The interest in sports which characterizes American life generally carries over into the relations of the alumnus to his college or university. It is not an altogether undesirable relationship.

But alumni loyalty moves beyond athletics. Partly it involves personal friendships. In coeducational colleges and universities, many a male student will have found his wife, and many a female student her husband. Their family relationship embraces the college or university where they met, and a certain loyalty endures while family life itself survives. Undergraduate and graduate life means other personal friendships as well, as some of these may continue beyond college life. Yet here again it is the bond of a common college career which links such friendships. To the extent that such friendships flourish, the college or university realizes an overflow of good will.

Undoubtedly, many alumni feel a particular sense of intellectual obligation to the college or university where they graduated. They realize that college provided them with the basis for their subsequent professional or other career. They remember a particularly stimulating professor who awakened a new insight into the world of the intellect. They recall some particular activity or enterprise from which they derived new meaning. They are thankful that their gropings toward maturity were treated with sympathy as well as firmness. Out of these accumulated memories, overcast with a nostalgia of innocent youth and carefree existence, the college or university builds a continuing tie of loyalty.

Perhaps to some extent there is an element of snobbishness in many college-alumnus relationships. The college lays claim upon the alumnus because it provided him something different from what he might have gotten anywhere else. The college cast him or her into a mold, a unique mold. This difference may be intellectual, or social, or a combination of both. It may be mostly imaginary. Yet it seems to exist, and it becomes meaningful to be able to say: "I am a Harvard man," or "a Princeton man," or "a Williams man," or "a Vassar woman," or "an Oberlin graduate." Whether the difference is real or not, many think it is real, and from this belief the rare flower of loyalty is husbanded.

What does the college or university expect from this loyalty? The easy answer is money. But this is the easy, and incomplete, answer. The principal hope of a college or university is that the alumnus will want to see his alma mater flourish. This means first of all a continuing interest in the intellectual standards of the college or university. The alumnus should know what the college or university stands for, what its educational objectives are, and what it is doing to realize its goals. The college or university cannot hope to be successful in the realization of its purposes without social support, and more than any place else it looks to its alumni for evidence of that sympathetic concern.

The college or university cannot hope to remain free unless alumni are interested in freedom. To college students freedom is a very real need. They are living in a period of transition from the supervision of parents to the supervision of other instruments of society: profession, community, their own family in which they are the principals. In this period the col-

lege or university does literally stand *in loco parentis.*
Students tend to resent this authority to which they
are subject, and the resentment often carries over into
a dull, continuing state of unanalyzed hostility.

It is one of the peculiar facts of the academic
community that students who are so interested in
freedom become alumni who are often so indifferent
or even hostile. Perhaps the articulate alumni are not
the same individuals as those who were articulate as
students. The alumni whose voices are heard are those
who attend alumni meetings, join the alumni association, read the alumni publications, and follow college
or university affairs. Alumni who are interested in
freedom must also have an associational life with the
college or university.

This freedom in which alumni must be interested has been mentioned before. There is first the
recognition that in social conflict the college or university as an entity is neutral. It does not take sides,
except in one respect. The college or university is
deeply committed to the proposition that reason must
be the major approach to every problem. And the
college or university believes in an orderly solution
to any social or other problem. Secondly, the individual faculty member must answer to his own conscience
for the fair, objective, and reasoned analysis of every
problem. In public discussion the faculty member
represents himself, not the college or university and
not the alumni. He may have deep-seated beliefs
about the problems of society, and like anyone else
he is free to express them. But the basic freedom of
the faculty member is to explore truth on a tentative

basis, and the basic freedom of the college or university is to provide the academic environment in which this faculty member's exploration may flourish.

To be sure, the freedom of the college or university in which the alumnus has an interest entails obligations as well. The college or university—both as community and as individuals—must emphasize its collective duty to be tolerant, reasonable, balanced in the consideration of any intellectual problem. The college or university cannot and should not attempt to withdraw from the society of which it is a part. But it must always clearly represent the part of society committed to reason in the discussion and solution of problems.

Alumni share this interest in freedom because as college graduates their distinctive social characteristic is education in ideas and in the process of orderly thought. Their contribution in society depends in good part upon the degree to which they do in fact possess knowledge, skill in the techniques of using knowledge, and ability to continue to grow in intelligence. These are characteristics made possible by a college education. These are characteristics which can be preserved and advanced only if the college or university is free to explore ideas.

The college or university hopes that its alumni will ever be ambassadors of higher learning in society. If our society as a whole lacks respect for college graduates, it will lack respect for colleges. If college graduates make no contribution to the general welfare, then a social concern for the welfare of higher education has little purpose. There will be a social disposition to assist colleges and universities only if their graduates demonstrate that society has benefited therefrom.

Each college or university is distinctive. It is, of course, possible to identify certain general trends in educational development of which most colleges or universities are representative. There were the colonial colleges and those which were created after 1790 modeled in large part upon these original colleges. There were the early state universities (in reality also colleges) encouraged by the Northwest Ordinance of 1787. There were the frontier colleges sponsored by various religious denominations. Subsequently, there were the state land-grant colleges assisted by the federal government's Morrill Acts of 1862 and 1890. There were the state normal and teachers colleges developed to help staff the expanding elementary and secondary schools of the land. There were the privately sponsored and the municipally sponsored colleges and universities established in the growing urban complexes. Colleges and universities throughout the land were established in one or more of these patterns to extend the opportunity for higher education.

The college or university expects its alumni to know something about the traditions of the particular school from which they have graduated. Each college or university wants its alumni to know something about the objectives it serves, to feel a sense of continuing loyalty to those objectives, and to work to see that those objectives, modified with changing circumstances, are pursued effectively.

Alumni power depends in large degree upon alumni understanding of the purposes of their particular college or university, its traditions, its organization, its support, its commitment to learning. When alumni possess and demonstrate a high regard for all these features of the academic community, they can influence both its social position and its internal operations. But this influence is resisted when alumni power appears to be primarily concerned with denying or subverting the basic goals of the academic community or with upsetting the delicate balance of its constituent elements and component programs. Alumni power is effective as it is moderate.

College and University Financial Support

Each college and university, almost without exception, looks to its alumni body for financial support. This financial assistance may come in one of three major ways. First, there is an organized alumni fund to which all alumni are annually asked to contribute. Usually the average of these gifts is relatively modest, ranging from $5 or $10 to as high as $200 or $300. Secondly, individual alumni may make one or more substantial gifts ($1,000 and over) during their lifetime and may provide a substantial bequest in their estates. Thirdly, alumni may encourage others to give, either through corporate, foundation, church, or personal channels. All such financial assistance is important to colleges and universities, whether privately or publicly sponsored.

At the present time, four-year colleges under private sponsorship tend to obtain about 65 per cent of their current operating educational and general income from student fees and the remaining from endowment income, annual gifts, and miscellaneous sources. A privately sponsored university may obtain as much as 40 per cent of its current income from research contracts of the federal government, about 30 per cent from student fees, and the remaining from endowment income and current gifts. A state university may obtain 60 per cent of its current educational income from state appropriations, 20 per cent from student fees, 14 per cent from federal research contracts and grants, and 6 per cent from endowment income and current gifts.

The point is that all colleges and universities depend upon gift income. The percentage may seem relatively modest, as in the instance of a state university. Yet in every case the amount is important, and each college or university is eager to increase the income received from gifts. And much of the increase will be expected from alumni sources. Alumni already contribute around 30 per cent of the gift income of a privately sponsored university and 20 per cent of the gift income of a public university. These proportions as well as the amounts they represent will advance, it is hoped, in the decade of the 1960s.

Money talks, and alumni power in any college or university invariably reflects in some degree the funds received from alumni. As colleges and universities obtain greater support from alumni, dependence upon alumni tends to become more pronounced. No college or university can afford to alienate any important segment of alumni who are contributing to its financial support. And similarly, no college or university desires purposefully to anger an individual alumnus who is active in raising money or is personally a large contributor.

It is impressive in experience to find that many wealthy alumni are content to give funds without trying at the same time to make the college or university over in their own image. Alumni are usually interested in education as such. They are not ready for their particular college or university to become completely an agency of government or an economic enterprise. They are willing to try to preserve some part of the philanthropic and religious nature of higher education, at least in the instance of the college or university from which they graduated. Alumni are eager to improve the quality of education provided to students and to enlarge the resources available for student aid. Ordinarily, no strings other than these two basic interests are attached to the bulk of alumni giving.

There are occasions when an alumnus or group of alumni will bring pressure to bear upon a college or university to discharge a particular professor or to alter a particular type of teaching. As active professional men and women, alumni are concerned about current social problems, whether these be the containment of communism, the desegregation of schools, or the relation of government to an expanding economy. It is often imagined—I say imagined advisedly —that some faculty member or group of faculty members is teaching students that the containment of communism is impractical or unnecessary, that permitting Negro children to go to school with white children is necessary to fulfill moral or cultural commitments of our society, or that government fiscal policy should play a positive role in promoting conditions of economic growth.

I have no desire here to debate the intellectual aspects of these current social problems. They are problems, and they are problems concerning which our knowledge is by no means complete or clear. It would seem clear, however, that the role of a college or university is to provide an environment in which these and other problems can be discussed fully, dispassionately, and tentatively. To the extent that knowledge can illuminate these issues, knowledge is always welcome. To the extent that research can provide additional knowledge and insight, research must be undertaken. To the extent that students can be helped to analyze issues, their education is essential.

If alumni are often critical of the academic community in its consideration of social controversy, the fault often rests with other groups in the academic community. Students, faculty members, and administration have not made it clear that their purpose is to promote discussion, the application of knowledge, and moral persuasion. Moreover, faculty and students desire to participate in the consideration of social issues in an active, not a passive, sense. The academic community does not encourage its students when they become alumni to withdraw from life. Rather, it encourages responsible participation. Yet the academic community is essentially fair-minded. It is this characteristic which alumni sometimes forget or come to believe has changed.

Money cannot be used to foreclose discussion. It can be used to enlarge discussion. Here the alumnus has especially important assistance to render, when he is willing to do so.

Alumni financial support can do much for higher education. How much it will accomplish in terms of basic goals will depend upon the wisdom and forbearance of alumni themselves. In the past the alumni record has been a good one indeed, and there is reason to expect that it will continue to be.

Conclusion

Alumni as college graduates are an essential constituent element of the academic community. The college graduate represents a continuing concern by a college lest the benefits of education be lost. The college graduate represents the group in society most concerned to preserve and defend the values of higher education. The college graduate represents a source of support for the well-being of colleges and universities.

Sometimes the insistence of alumni may prevent necessary changes in a college or university program, or location, or clientele because of a desire to preserve a familiar past. Sometimes the insistence of alumni may fail to support a college or university in its efforts to advance the quality of its activities.

Alumni are a very real power in the academic community. Sometimes alumni do not live up to their high obligation. Sometimes alumni are in the forefront of efforts to strengthen and expand educational efforts. The alumnus may influence the academic community to the extent that he understands it, sympathizes with its objectives, criticizes it with constructive intent, and supports it.

Chapter 6

Administration

THE FOURTH CONSTITUENT ELEMENT of the academic community is administration. In a private business enterprise the corresponding group would be collectively termed "management." The label "administration" is more appropriate for a college or university, because the task of administration is to facilitate, not to manage, the preservation, transmission, and advancement of knowledge.

Perhaps no part of the academic community is more often misunderstood, or criticized, especially by faculty and students, than administration. The power invested in administration is frequently exaggerated. The prestige and status of administration are believed to be substantial. The limitations of both power and status are usually poorly defined, yet quite real. These factors contribute to a general misunderstanding which can be harmful to the orderly operation of a college or university.

The facts actually are these. Administration is essential to the maintenance of the academic com-

179

munity as an environment of learning. A college or university cannot function, or would not long be able to, without the specialized and full-time endeavor of those who seek to free the energies of faculty and students for the pursuit of learning. Administration exists not to dominate faculty or students but to serve them. The restraints imposed are, or should be, those which are the minimum requirements of an organized society having common purposes and common needs. Many of the restraints are economic, arising from the availability of limited resources for educational purposes. Other restraints are social, arising from the necessity of restricting the freedom of some in order to advance the freedom of others. Still additional restraints are institutional, to make certain that learning comes first and that the good repute of higher education is not tarnished.

The Functions of Administration

Administration in the academic community must perform three essential functions. These are (1) to provide educational leadership and to cultivate an image of the college or university; (2) to augment and to allocate the scarce economic resources of the college or university; and (3) to maintain the college or university as a going, viable enterprise. Each of these functions requires some elaboration.

Two considerations deserve emphasis at the outset of this discussion. First, the power vested in administration is limited to that required for the performance of these functions. It may even be asserted that this power is the minimum extent of authority essential to the realization of these purposes. Secondly, this power of administration by its very nature must necessarily come into conflict with faculty, student, and alumni power. I shall have more to say about conflict in the next chapter. Here I would point out only that the power of administration must be cautiously and carefully exercised, since its pervasive nature is such that, pushed to its extreme, it can well deny the exercise of power by faculty, students, and alumni. In other words, administration power to be acceptable to the academic community and to realize its actual purpose must be considered a limited power.

The concept of community within the institution of higher education cannot survive if the power of administration is thought of as a supreme echelon in a hierarchy of authority. If the concept of hierarchy is accepted within a college or university, then administration becomes the fount of authority from which faculty, students, and alumni draw their respective roles, and under whose direction and control all activity is performed. Such a concept of authority, it seems to me, is alien to the great social purpose of higher education and does not conform with the facts of academic life. On the other hand, when the power of administration is conceived as a constituent element of a community of power, then the functions of that power are more definitely prescribed and the limitations of that power are more clearly understood.

The Structure of Administrative Power— Trustees

Just as faculty power is structured in terms of disciplines and professional fields of knowledge, and in terms of departments, colleges and schools, and a university (not to mention centers and institutes), so administration power is structured. There are at least three major groupings of persons in this structure. The first is a board of trustees. The second is a president and his academic staff. The third is a president and his auxiliary staff.

It is customary in the literature of higher education to present boards of trustees as enjoying the final and complete authority of governance within a college or university. Then, just as soon as this statement is made, it is almost always followed immediately by an admonition to the effect that trustees will be well advised to avoid the exercise of complete authority. Indeed, it is commonly said that by a great act of self-denial boards of trustees in the United States have refrained from controlling educational policy and the instructional process, from specifying detailed requirements of student behavior, from directing alumni activity.[1]

[1] For statements about the authority and proper role of trustees, see among others Raymond M. Hughes, *A Manual for Trustees of Colleges and Universities* (Ames, Iowa: The Iowa State College Press, 1943); Ordway Tead, *Trustees— Teachers—Students* (Salt Lake City, Utah: University of Utah Press, 1951); and Morton A. Rauh, *College and University Trusteeship* (Yellow Springs, Ohio: The Antioch Press, 1959).

For legal reasons, and in terms of the necessity of maintaining the existence of a college or a university as a continuing corporate entity, the power of trustees may be stated in very broad terms indeed.[2] The legal prescription, however, must be interpreted in the light of the objectives of higher education as an institution and in the recognition of the reality of faculty, student, and alumni power. The actions of trustees tend in general to reflect an understanding of this fact of limited power.

The position of a board of trustees seems to me to be essentially one of oversight of the administration of a college or university. The board is deeply concerned with educational leadership, not because it is competent to provide such leadership but because it realizes the tendency of a profession to become dedicated to tradition, to engage in introspection, and to subscribe to ingrown practices. The board is deeply concerned with the expansion and utilization of economic resources. The board is deeply concerned with the efficient and effective performance of the services needed to maintain the college or university as an ongoing community.

In a sense it might be said that the board of trustees is the keeper of the social conscience, the protector of the public interest in higher education. The board is a peculiar kind of representative device. In the political institutions of American society, the legislature determines the public policy which expresses

---

[2] See Thomas Edward Blackwell, *College Law: A Guide for Administrators* (Washington, D.C.: American Council on Education, 1961).

the public interest in governmental activity. In this political process, the legislature is guided by executive leadership, administrative advice, and the pressures of interest groups. The board of trustees of a college or university, whether publicly or privately sponsored, is an insulating arrangement standing between the political process as spokesman of the public interest and the faculty, students, and alumni as spokesmen of their particular interests.

It must be noted that the board of trustees of a privately sponsored college or university is equally guardian of the public interest in higher education as is the board of trustees of a publicly sponsored college or university. The privately sponsored college or university is the recipient of public funds and public tax exemptions, along with the publicly sponsored college or university. The boards of private colleges and universities have a public interest to maintain and preserve.

The public interest in higher education must be insulated from the ordinary political process because we recognize that majorities in a democratic political system may be misguided in their judgment at a particular time in a particular place about the true nature of the public interest. I have commented several times about the peculiar social nature of higher education, dedicated as it is in Western society to the advancement of knowledge and to the enlargement of knowledge available to the individual and to society for their use. This purpose of higher education may come under attack in the midst of social conflict in our society. The board of trustees is a device for filtering the immediate demands of a militant majority which might wish to curtail the advancement and transmission of knowledge.

At the same time, the board of trustees is a reminder to faculty, students, and alumni of an interest beyond their own particular group in the functioning of higher education. There is more than a faculty interest in higher education. There is more than a student interest in higher education. There is more than an alumni interest in higher education. Beyond this there is a public interest as well. Perhaps public interest is an outworn concept. Perhaps it has no meaning in any rational or ideal sense.[3] The moral imperative of life cannot be set aside simply because it cannot be validated by scientific procedure.

In the performance of this public interest function, the board of trustees will necessarily rely heavily upon the president of the college or university. This is just one reason why the selection and support of a president is such an important task for a board of trustees. The board may need to be reminded by the president of its high calling. In turn, the board may have to serve as arbiter in conflict between faculty, students, alumni, and the administrative staff of the college or university. The board must also evaluate continually the performance of administration as a constituent part of the academic community. If this evaluation is unfavorable, there is little choice except to ask a president to resign. The board must then find another president.

[3] See Glendon Schubert, *The Public Interest* (Glencoe, Ill.: Free Press, 1960).

Boards of trustees have a number of formal actions to take: to approve faculty recommendations on academic policy, to approve essentials of student conduct, to approve an operating budget and a capital budget, to borrow funds, to raise fees charged students, to seek additional sources of income, to accept gifts, to manage endowment funds, and to establish rules and procedures to perpetuate the body corporate of the college or university. In the publicly sponsored university it may be a body politic as well to preserve. In all these actions a board may act almost as a matter of routine. If too many details require board action, routine is almost certain to become the only avenue of escape from complete paralysis.

Boards of trustees are well advised to give attention to the broad implications of the detail which comes to their attention. A board needs to bear always in mind that its role is not to handle detail but to see in detail issues of importance which require careful consideration. To these a board brings its particular talent: the talent of conscience, the talent of the lighthouse above the waves of momentary storm, the talent of a peak above the ordinary heights of man. The board of trustees provides a collective expression of value judgments drawn from beyond the academic community itself.

The Structure of Administrative Power—the President

The president of a college or university serves in a dual capacity. Formally, he is selected by the board of trustees and is responsible to them. He is the chief administrative officer of the college or university, exercising general oversight of the functions of administration within the academic community. But the president is also more than this. He is the principal member of the faculty, first among equals, the educational leader.

There is a feeling that in recent years in particular the role of the president as an educational leader has suffered some eclipse.[4] If this has occurred, and certainly there is evidence to justify such a point of view, a number of reasons would explain this development. No doubt faculties have become more and more powerful in the academic community with the expansion and increasing specialization of knowledge and with the growing importance of research as an academic activity. No one person can hope to be acquainted with the details of the disciplines and the professional fields. Unfortunately, few scholars emerging from their particular field of learning have acquired the ability to be generalists in higher education. Furthermore, boards of trustees have tended in recent years to give too much attention to the prospective administrative ability of a possible president and too little attention to his role as an educational leader. And undoubtedly, the administrative burdens of the college and university president have become heavier than ever before.

[4] This is stated very forcibly in the volume by former President Harold W. Dodds of Princeton, entitled *The Academic President—Educator or Caretaker?* (New York: The McGraw-Hill Book Company, Inc., 1962).

Former President Dodds of Princeton argues that at least 50 per cent of a president's time should be devoted to educational matters. To be sure, in the broadest sense of the word, every problem confronting administration in the academic community is an educational problem. President Dodds uses the word to refer to such matters as curriculum and course requirements, faculty instructional loads, faculty research, faculty appointments, instructional procedures, and professional standards. All these are vital concerns.

To some extent faculties probably resent the leadership role of a president because he is chosen by the board of trustees rather than by the faculty itself. This initial hostility can be overcome in part at least if the board arranges for consultation with a faculty committee during the selection process. This hostility can also be partially avoided if the person chosen has had faculty as well as administrative experience. Indeed, I would argue emphatically that every college or university president should have been a faculty member at some time in his career. It is difficult for me to understand the general acceptance of the proposition that a superintendent of schools should at one time have been a classroom teacher and the reluctant acceptance of the proposition by many that a president of a college or university ought to have been a faculty member. Surely the requirements for a superintendent of schools are not more rigorous than those for a college or university president.

I doubt whether faculties always appreciate the

advantages of having a president selected by a board of trustees, or the service rendered by boards in undertaking such selection. Arrangements for the choice of leaders have been a social problem throughout recorded history. Neither philosophers nor statesmen have been able to devise a perfect system. Leadership status may be hereditary, but this affords no guarantee of ability. Leadership may be won by conquest or the power of might in each generation, but such a system is scarcely conducive to social cohesion or peaceful existence. Leadership may be vested in a guild or closed corporation. Plato envisaged such an arrangement of philosopher-kings, but he could only hope that each group would select youth to succeed it solely upon the basis of ability and not because of family connections, family wealth, or other such factors. Leadership may be based upon election, but this results in either the politics of acquiescence or the politics of manipulation. Neither situation is altogether desirable in the academic community.[5]

Leadership based upon trustee selection is leadership founded upon the best judgment of an objective and conscientious group of persons. At least this is the ideal. And anyone would be hard pressed to maintain that any other known system for the identification and selection of leaders would guarantee better results. One is tempted to say that on the whole American college and university presidents have done a fairly decent job under very trying circumstances, and

[5] Faculty members enamored of the idea of faculty election of presidents would do well to read C. P. Snow's brilliant novel, *The Masters* (New York: The Macmillan Company, 1951).

that the judgment of boards of trustees has been as good as might be expected of any other group of men in our society.

As educational leader, the president is presiding officer of the faculty in its collective activities. He can exercise such leadership in these collective endeavors as he is willing to assert. He needs to understand, however, just what is the collective role of the faculty —that is, what is the power of the faculty as a whole. An invasion of power reserved for the individual faculty member or the department may readily arouse resentment, and with justification.

To repeat, the president's position as an educational leader is one of leadership at the level of the faculty in its collective capacity. The president can and should endeavor to provide a sense of purpose and principle to the entire faculty. He should facilitate but not dominate the process of faculty decision making. He should protect the individual, the department, and the school from any temptation to collective tyranny by the faculty as a whole.

Furthermore, the president must watch to make certain that the best collective judgment of the faculty is carried out in the administrative activity of the academic community. The president enjoys the great advantage of combining in his person the role of faculty leader and the role of chief administrative officer. The two are not positions of conflict but rather positions of mutual compatibility. In this way faculty judgment as officially voiced or as interpreted according to the "sense of the meeting" can be given effect in the performance of the tasks of administration.

The Structure of Administrative Power—the Administrative Staff

Just as the president serves in a dual capacity of educational leader and chief administrative officer, so he has a dual group of associates who make up the administrative organization of the academic community. This organization will be elaborate or simple, depending upon the size of the academic community and upon the extent of its educational activities. This organization will vary also with the extent to which faculty and administrative activities have been centralized or decentralized in schools and departments.

Ordinarily a president is aided in his role of educational leader by a dean of the faculty in a college, or by a provost or vice president for academic affairs in a university. On occasion in some of our large universities there is also a vice president for medical affairs. This arrangement recognizes the special importance, and the expense, of medical education and research in the university, activities which may require the central attention of someone professionally qualified in the field of medicine. Large universities have also been tending to establish a vice president for research, recognizing the magnitude of specially budgeted research, mostly under federal government contracts and grants. The deans of instructional colleges and universities also constitute a part of the machinery of academic affairs in a university.

The result is that in a university in particular, but to some extent in a college as well, educational leadership is a collegial task. The president presides over what is in effect an educational council where major issues of educational policy and procedure are resolved, always subject to faculty approval or support.

In addition to these arrangements for educational leadership, there are a number of centralized educational services to operate in a college or university. The most important of these remains the library. But other services are rapidly coming to the fore in our universities especially: radio and broadcasting service, audio-visual service, and institutional research concerning the learning process and utilization of learning resources. The service of student admission and the service of central student record keeping may be considered student services or educational services. They have characteristics of both, but I am disposed to classify them as educational services. In any event, the various central educational services just mentioned must be supervised in a general way by the educational leadership of a college or university.

Secondly, there is a vast range of activities known as student affairs, or student personnel services. These are often brought together under a dean of students or a vice president for student affairs. The president must give some attention to this area of administrative effort, where the social, health, living, and other general problems of students receive guidance and assistance.

Thirdly, there are the so-called "business affairs"

of a college or university. They embrace a varied array of activity, from building construction and operation, security, purchasing, reproduction and printing, transportation service, and communication service to the appointment of nonacademic personnel, accounting, the collection of accounts, the management of residence halls, insurance, and the handling of investments. The operation of these services may be handled by a vice president for business affairs or they may be separately organized under a business manager and a treasurer.

Finally, there is the general field of activity known as public relations and development. Here the concern is to create a favorable image of the college or university and to cultivate all available sources of financial support. Public information, alumni relations, fund raising—these activities are closely interrelated. Here again in our large universities there is a tendency to bring all these efforts together under a vice president for development or an assistant to the president for public relations.

Here in outline is the general internal structure of the administration element of the academic community. These are all activities without which faculty, students, and alumni would be unable to fulfill their roles in higher education.

It would require an entire volume to describe all the various services and operations of administration in a college or university. It may be worthwhile, however, simply in order to underline the importance of administration in the academic community, to mention certain aspects of some of these areas of activity.

Physical Plant

The expansion of physical plant at American colleges and universities has been proceeding at a substantial rate. In the five years from 1951 through 1955, total construction is reported to have exceeded 1.75 billion dollars.[6] Some 800 million dollars were expended for instructional facilities, about 100 million dollars for research plant, nearly 500 million dollars for residential facilities, and the remaining 400 million dollars for general purposes (administration, athletics, student centers, power plants, chapels, auditoriums, faculty clubs, and student hospitals).

It is interesting to observe the source of financing for this volume of construction. For the publicly sponsored universities and colleges, about 55 per cent of the some 1 billion dollars of building came from governmental sources, some 35 per cent from borrowed funds (especially from revenue bonds), and the remaining 10 per cent from gifts and current funds.[7] For the privately sponsored colleges and universities, over 56 per cent of the construction was made possible by gifts, about 30 per cent by borrowed funds (including investment of own funds), and the remaining 14 per cent by current funds and government grants.[8]

[6] W. Robert Bokelman and John B. Rork, *College and University Facilities Survey,* part 1: Cost and Financing of College and University Buildings, 1951–55, U.S. Office of Education Circular no. 540, 1959.

[7] *Ibid.,* table 21.

[8] *Ibid.,* table 21.

Moreover, the estimates of construction needed during the decade of the 1960s are large.[9] The needs for instructional, research, and general plant are estimated to range from 4.5 to 6.5 billion dollars, while the needs for residence hall plant are estimated to range from 2 to 3 billion dollars. The total is a staggering 6.5 to 9.5 billion dollars. If these goals are to be realized, we shall have to increase the rate of construction growth at American colleges and universities by 50 to 150 per cent above that which actually occurred from 1951 through 1955.

Few problems agitate an academic community more than architectural style, the division and use of building funds, and the design of physical facilities. Faculty members hold strong points of view about buildings. Not only are they concerned about office space, laboratory facilities, classrooms, seminar rooms, and meeting rooms, but also they seem to expect parking space on top of or below every academic structure.[10] Alumni are concerned about uniformity of architectural style, symmetry of building placement, attractive appearance, well-kept lawns, and preservation of monuments. Students seem to be especially interested in adequate places to eat and sleep and telephones for everyone, although occasionally one hears complaints about insufficient study space.

[9] See John D. Long, *Needed Expansion of Facilities for Higher Education—1958–70: How Much Will It Cost?* (Washington, D.C.: American Council on Education, 1958).

[10] For an expression of faculty viewpoint, see William Bruce Cameron and Raymond H. Wheeler, "Physical Setting and Intellectual Climate," *School and Society,* vol. 89 (Feb. 25, 1961), p. 75.

Two aspects of physical plant planning are often overlooked or slighted in discussions of the subject. One is the great backlog of plant need which has developed in most colleges and universities. Construction was largely halted from 1930 to 1946 at many colleges and universities, except for projects that the publicly sponsored colleges and universities were able to undertake with the matching federal government grants under the public works program. After World War II, colleges and universities had to catch up with the deferred construction and the advancing obsolescence of existing plant while endeavoring to increase facilities to meet first the veterans' bulge and then an expanding student enrollment. Under these circumstances scarcely a building could be completed which was not too small or otherwise inadequate when finished. The other problem has been one of balance in the development of physical facilities. To faculty members, student residences and other student facilities seem of secondary importance, while such needs as utilities, storage facilities, and administration buildings are inconsequential. Yet all these facilities in some degree of balance one with the other are essential to the development of a college or university campus.

Another factor which complicates the construction of physical facilities is the varied sources from which capital funds may be derived. Often one type of financing is available for only one kind of structure and not for another. This differentiation is not always clearly understood by the various constituent elements of the academic community. For example, construction grants have been available through federal government agencies for research facilities in the physical and biological sciences, but not for instruction facilities in these fields. No construction grants have been available for research facilities in the social sciences. Similarly, since 1950 and especially since the interest formula was altered in 1955, federal loans on generous terms have been available for the construction of residence halls. Such loans have not been available for academic facilities, nor are they equally useful for privately and publicly sponsored colleges and universities. Indeed, in most states the public university would not be able under present laws and present financial practices to make any use of loans for academic facilities.

Often an individual donor specifies that his gift shall be used for a chapel, for a laboratory, for a library, or for some other particular purpose. Sometimes a member of the faculty has close relationships with a person of wealth and is able to interest him in a certain kind of gift. The object of such benevolence may not always be the most needed facility at the moment on a campus. Yet when a gift is made for a designated kind of structure, the administration of a college or university has no choice upon acceptance of the gift except to carry out the specific wishes of the donor.

Plant planning has become a matter of great importance. Statements of need must be developed in detail and with considerable care, especially in the publicly sponsored universities where requests may be reviewed by the state's capital improvement and planning board.[11] Necessarily faculty members must be expected to provide the general outline of facility requirements, such as classroom sizes and equipment, laboratory sizes and equipment, office space, and immediate service needs. Buildings are after all intended to facilitate the instructional and research program of the college or university.

A statement of requirements, however, is only one part of plant planning. Architectural style, campus location, and financing must be considered. These factors may have their impact upon space requirements and upon one another. To administration falls the task of endeavoring to reconcile these various considerations. Compromise is the inevitable result, except when the wishes of a donor override all other factors. The process is likely to please no one completely.

There is little point in discussing architectural style. The central issue in college and university planning is whether to preserve continuity of style or to let buildings reflect the prevailing architectural ideas of the time when they are constructed. There are some possibilities of compromise between these two positions, but compromise usually reveals itself as just that. Individuals react to architectural style even as to paintings, music, interior decoration, and other art forms. In the end a board of trustees is usually expected to express a generalized judgment about which program of style to pursue.

[11] See William T. Middlebrook, *How to Estimate the Building Needs of a College or University* (Minneapolis: University of Minnesota Press, 1958).

The importance of balance in plant planning deserves mention again. When one thinks of academic plant, does one's concern extend also to space for such services as printing, reproduction, automotive maintenance, campus mail, cold storage, tabulating, accounting, repair of scientific apparatus, and military storage? All these needs are included in the calculation of space for internal services in a large state-sponsored university.[12] It is easy to overlook them or to believe that they are unimportant to the functioning of a college or university.

Indeed, the figures on percentage distribution of building space at a great university, *excluding* housing facilities, are somewhat startling. In the study of operating costs and statistics carried on by the universities of the Western Conference and the University of California, an analysis was included on the distribution of space for various purposes.[13] One private college of liberal arts was included in the study, as well as various campuses of the University of California. It was found that the proportion of space utilized for instruction, including teaching laboratories, ranged from 14 to 38 per cent. Research laboratories required from 3 to 26 per cent of available space. Office facilities occupied from 10 to 21 per cent. Libraries and museums occupied from 3 to 17 per cent. Space for general uses, such as theaters, gymnasiums, and armories, took from 3 to 30 per cent.

[12] *Ibid.,* pp. 41–47.
[13] *California and Western Conference Cost and Statistical Study for the Year 1954–1955* (Berkeley, Calif.: University of California Press, 1959), table 20.

General services required from 6 to 40 per cent of available space. It was obvious that no such thing as a pattern of common usage of space could be found among these particular campuses. If student residence space had been included in the analysis, the proportions devoted to the uses just enumerated would have been even lower.

In plant planning it is highly desirable to give the educational services an opportunity to contribute to the outline of desirable room specifications. Departments which make extensive use of audio-visual methods are likely to set forth classroom requirements without any mention of instructional practices. It is often assumed that administrative officials will see to it that needs for projection equipment and other special features are included.

The buildings maintenance staff has important contributions also to make to plant planning. No persons are more familiar with the deficiencies of existing facilities than those who operate and maintain them. Ideas about wiring, plumbing, floor covering, lighting, ventilation, and acoustics can be obtained from the maintenance staff. These are ideas which deserve careful consideration.

Administration necessarily gives a great deal of attention to the development of a capital plant plan. Partly this is a matter of necessity. Partly it is a matter of specialization within the academic community. Perhaps the two factors are so highly interrelated as to be one. Administration is the agency of the academic community which must evaluate competing plant requirements. If the faculty as a legislative assembly were to undertake the determination of a capital plan and its priorities, the result might well be the kind of collection of items for everyone with which we are familiar in the public works legislation of federal and state governments. A department or school is well aware of its own immediate needs for new or improved physical facilities but is less concerned about the needs of other departments and schools. Sometimes a department is critical of the space use proposed by another department. I have known one department to criticize another department for wanting a museum. Administration must serve as an impartial arbitrator of these differences.

Moreover, because plant planning requires such detailed and specialized preparation, some full-time and even professional attention must be given to the details of the task. The function of planning falls into the hands of administration without much argument, and administration in consequence gives a great deal of time and energy to the activity. Necessarily, in so far as possible administration must endeavor to satisfy the competing needs of the various parts of the academic community in such a way as to preserve a sense of balance and fairness. The educational objectives of a college or university are reflected in its capital plan and in the priorities which are established for its realization. All parts of the academic community are vitally concerned in such a development plan.

Student Personnel Services

One of the major trends in college and university administration in the past twenty years has been the elaboration of the student personnel program. Student personnel services today embrace such activities as aptitude counseling and assistance, health service, housing and food service, supervision of social activities, financial and employment aid, enforcement of conduct rules, advice to foreign students, administration of veterans' regulations, encouragement of religious activities, general orientation, and placement.[14] I omit from this listing the work of admissions and student record keeping.

There was a time when student personnel work was almost nonexistent, or at best embryonic. Faculty members themselves lived in student residence halls, where these existed, or residence supervision was meager. Health was a concern for the individual student and his family. Social activities were little supervised. Conduct regulations were often detailed and strict, but the faculty was expected to ensure their enforcement. Such counseling and placement assistance as the student received came from faculty members. Little concern was given to student aid; there

[14] From Daniel D. Feder et al., *The Administration of Student Personnel Programs in American Colleges and Universities,* the nineteenth and concluding brochure in a series of studies on student personnel work published between 1939 and 1958 (Washington, D.C.: American Council on Education, 1958). All nineteen pamphlets constitute a general treatise on student personnel work.

might be a scholarship and loan officer, often a member of the faculty serving on a part-time basis, but scholarships were awarded strictly on the basis of academic performance and loans were relatively unimportant until after 1930. It was the aftermath of World War II which produced the problems of assistance to veterans and foreign students.

For the most part colleges and universities have tended in recent years to expand their student personnel services and to recruit a professionally educated staff specializing in the various phases of such activity.[15] Several different forces have conjoined to bring about this development. One factor appears to be the increasing proportion of young people going to college and the need to assist them in defining their educational abilities and interests. Another factor has been the expansion of high school education so that college preparation is no longer the principal objective of secondary schooling. Many college students have not been ready for college study without assistance in study habits and reading aptitude. The larger number of college students has brought new problems in social supervision and discipline. Health has become a group rather than an individual concern.

[15] See E. G. Williamson, ed., *Trends in Student Personnel Work* (Minneapolis: University of Minnesota Press, 1949); C. Gilbert Wrenn, *Student Personnel Work in College* (New York: The Ronald Press Company, 1951); Esther Lloyd-Jones and Margaret Ruth Smith, eds., *Student Personnel Work as Deeper Teaching* (New York: Harper & Brothers, 1954); and Margaret B. Fisher and Jeanne L. Noble, *College Education as Personal Development* (Englewood Cliffs, N.J.: Prentice-Hall, Inc., 1960).

I am disposed to think that there is another important force at work here. Faculty members have tended to withdraw from direct contact with students except in the classroom and in the office where an immediate academic problem is involved. The growth of research by faculty members and the increased effort demanded in preparing lectures and other class materials have given faculty members less time and inclination to worry about the personal problems of students. In addition, the emergence of both a specialized point of view and a specialized competence in working with students has encouraged the growth of student personnel work. Most faculty members now defer to this special competence and acknowledge that they have little basis in knowledge or experience for handling the complex social problems of present-day students.

Student personnel work begins with a commitment. It is that students can be guided through discussion, counseling, and other forms of assistance to make important decisions affecting both their academic and personal lives. The student personnel point of view is nonauthoritarian. It is essentially permissive, reinforced by modern techniques of presenting factual and other information for the guidance of student choice. This is a patient, time-consuming process. It is almost fair to say that the student personnel staff on a college or university campus is the one group with time, or willing to make time, to listen to students.

Student personnel work conceives of its role as

supplementary or complementary to the formal academic learning process. Indeed, it may be argued that
students learn as much from their social and practical
activity (journalistic, dramatic, musical, etc.) as they
do from their classroom and laboratory work. The
student personnel staff seeks to guide much of this
endeavor, which is especially extensive on the residential campus. Even directors of student centers
conceive of their purpose as in good part intellectual,
through musical, art, and similar programs.

Then there is a vast amount of detailed activity
to be performed today which did not exist a generation ago. For example, student financial aid has
become a highly specialized function. Scholarships are
in large part awarded on the basis of a calculation
involving academic promise *and* financial need. Federal government participation in the loan program
has brought vast new record keeping. Moreover, student financial assistance now sets as its goal a tailoring
of scholarship, loan, and employment forms of aid to
suit individual circumstances. It is the formal policy
of some colleges and universities to insist upon a combination of types of assistance in many cases.

Placement activity has become another specialized service. The advent of modern personnel systems
in large business corporations and in public schools
has had its impact upon the college or university
campus. The personnel recruiter expects to have
interviews arranged and records of prospective employees prepared in one place and by one person.
Whether placement is organized on a university-wide

basis or on a professional school basis, there is still a specialized function to perform which requires a good deal of time.

Presumably there are two choices available to a college or university in setting forth its social philosophy for undergraduate students. One choice is to say that the social life of the student is of little direct concern to the college or university. So long as the student meets the academic standards of the academic community and abides by the general standards of conduct enforced by the external community, the student may behave socially as he pleases. The other choice is to say that the academic community has a special responsibility *in loco parentis* to exercise a definite and continuing oversight of social conduct by students. The student in terms of age and maturity is not yet to be regarded as an adult responsible personally for his own conduct but must continue to receive guidance and direction in his social behavior. Accordingly, the use of automobiles, the consumption of alcoholic beverages, the hours and places of social gatherings for men and women students, and other types of behavior are subject to defined restrictions.

The first attitude enforces an academic standard of conduct only. The other enforces a social standard of conduct as a reinforcement of the academic standard. No doubt the relative merits of each point of view might be argued at great length. Few if any careful studies have been made of the consequences of either upon the academic and post-college achievement of students. Within the wide range of varied practices which characterize colleges and universities in the United States, one may find different versions of each attitude toward students. Both the individual academic community and the individual student must decide which point of view to adopt or accept.

In any event, some degree of student personnel work is now characteristic of almost all colleges and universities. It is another part of the task now commonly regarded as entrusted to college and university administration as distinct from the faculty and student body themselves.

Business Services

The various so-called "business services" are essential to the operation of the academic community.[16] The idea of central purchasing, storage, and distribution of supplies and equipment, for example, is generally accepted in colleges and universities today. This means that specialized personnel and facilities are devoted to the function of buying and handling the supplies and equipment required by a college or university. This procurement activity is extensive indeed on a campus, ranging from soap and paper napkins to chemistry supplies and electronic equipment. Faculty members must be relied upon to outline specifications, to estimate quantities needed, and

[16] These and certain financial services as well are discussed in *College and University Business Administration,* vol. II, compiled by the National Committee on the Preparation of a Manual on College and University Business Administration (Washington, D.C.: American Council on Education, 1955).

even to suggest suppliers, but the actual process of purchasing, arranging delivery, and handling payment is a technical one. Moreover, a central stores operation is necessary in order to provide consumable supplies on a continuing flow basis.

Similar comments may be made about the maintenance and operation of buildings. This again is a highly technical specialization, particularly in such matters as the provision of electrical service, the operation of a central heating plant, and the assurance of water and sanitary sewer service. The operation of a dining hall embraces many activities, from food procurement and preparation to the establishment of dietary standards, the enforcement of health standards, and the maintenance of careful cost controls.

Modern personnel management recognizes the importance of establishing and observing common work specifications and pay classifications for similar categories of employment, from custodians of buildings to typists and stenographers, from bookkeepers to machine operators, from laboratory technicians to cooks and bakers, from groundsmen to police officers.

Many colleges and universities have their own security force. The safeguarding of campus property is a full-time task. Moreover, in many communities students must be protected from undesirable intruders. And on occasion, unfortunately, it is necessary to quell or discourage student demonstrations. Many local communities are reluctant to assume responsibility for police or fire protection of a college or university because they receive no tax support from the property of the college or university. In turn, administrative officers of many colleges and universities have learned from the accumulated experience of centuries to rely upon their own resources for protection rather than upon a local community; in this way some of the inevitable animosity between town and gown can be mitigated.

Enough has been said to suggest both the range and the importance of the business services which are provided in an academic community. Their satisfactory performance is essential to the success of instruction and research in a college or university.

Financial Management

Even though the current income and expenditures of nearly two thousand colleges (junior and senior) and universities are around 6 billion dollars a year (1961–1962), this amount is not adequate for accomplishing the objectives of higher education in the United States. Six billion dollars will not provide the quantity and quality of instruction and research which most colleges and universities would like to realize. Even in those instances where expansion of enrollment is not a major purpose of a college or university, the academic community would like to pay higher salaries and so attract and retain abler scholars, or it would like to spend more money on faculty research, or it would like to have new instructional equipment, or it would like to spend more for student aid.

The administration of a college or university begins with the basic proposition that current financial resources are never sufficient to do all the things the academic community desires. Thus the first objective of financial management is to augment scarce resources. There may be an eventual limit to the financial needs of higher education, and perhaps to the income requirements of a particular college or university. But such a salubrious situation seems too remote at the moment to require consideration.

Various policy problems and procedures are involved in augmenting income. To what extent should students be expected to provide the income needed by a college or university? Shall philanthropy be sought as endowment capital or current income? Shall philanthropy be obtained through alumni as individuals, through churches, through corporations, through civic bodies? Shall government assistance be sought from local government, from state government, from the federal government? Shall government financial assistance be confined to student aid and research? Shall government aid be sought primarily through tax exemption (which is enjoyed by all colleges and universities) or through direct receipts? These are just examples of the issues at stake.

Colleges and universities ordinarily divide their income and expenditures into three major categories: educational and general, auxiliary services, and student aid.[17] The activities carried on under each of these headings are fundamentally different; they raise

[17] See *College and University Business Administration,* vol. I, compiled by the National Committee on the Preparation of a Manual on College and University Administration (Washington, D.C.: American Council on Education, 1952).

different issues of financing. For example, should auxiliary services such as residence halls, student centers, and student health services be supported on the basis of direct costs or on the basis of direct *and* indirect costs? Should expenditures for student aid be limited to income received directly for this purpose, or should general income be used for student aid?

This is at best an inadequate outline of the financial issues confronting a college or university. Moreover, it gives no idea of the immense amount of time which a state university president and his financial staff must give to the preparation of detailed budget estimates, the calculation of unit expenditures, the comparison of expenditure data with other universities, and the justification of levels of expenditure. Much time must be given to budget hearings in the budget office and before legislative committees. Similarly, the president and staff of a privately sponsored college or university will often devote much effort to increasing philanthropic support, with all of the attendant cultivation of potential donors.

Even where faculty members themselves are instrumental in obtaining financial resources, problems are presented for administration to resolve. When a faculty member interests some person in making a gift, there are questions about the housing and continuing support of equipment or materials. If the gift is cash for instruction or research, there are questions of handling the funds to be settled. When a faculty member obtains a research grant from a foundation or a government agency, there are problems of handling the necessary overhead in plant and administrative costs. A university president may find himself seeking funds simply to keep the university in operation to handle all its research grants.

Usually, it is university administration which is expected to augment income to carry on instruction and research, student aid, and all the necessary services. Most colleges and universities are continually striving to increase income from all available sources, especially from students, government, and philanthropy. Different patterns of support emerge in the college and the university, in the residential and the nonresidential college or university, and in the privately and the publicly sponsored college or university. Most colleges and universities seek a diversity of financial support, while trying to convince faculty, students, and alumni that essential needs are being met.

Perhaps no issue is more troublesome for the administration of a publicly sponsored university than how far it should go in seeking income from students. The low-tuition principle has been a foundation stone of publicly sponsored higher education. That foundation is being steadily eroded by the difficulties state legislatures encounter in providing adequate financial support for state-sponsored colleges and universities. Yet the pressures for more income, especially to meet faculty salaries, are impossible for administration to ignore.

Perhaps no issue is more troublesome for the administration of a privately sponsored college or university to resolve than how far it should go in seeking and accepting income from government. And if government income shall be accepted, shall it be state and local government support or federal government support? And if government income shall be accepted, under what terms and conditions and for what purposes shall it be accepted? How far can a privately sponsored college or university go in accepting government support and still consider itself privately sponsored? How far can a church-related college or university go in accepting government support and still consider itself properly separated from government?

All these are weighty issues, and they are issues on which decisions based upon principle as well as expediency must be made. In the last analysis here again boards of trustees must make the final decision, based upon recommendations of the president who in turn must reflect the opinions of faculty and students as well as of philanthropists and legislators.

Then when resources are available they must be allocated for use. This involves the preparation of budgets for all parts of a college or university. I shall have more to say about this in the next chapter. There is not space to mention investment management of endowment funds or insurance management of property as still further aspects of the prudent administration of a college or university.

The purpose here is simply to outline the important range of financial problems to be decided in an academic community and to suggest that administration must exercise the authority to make final decisions. Faculty, students, and alumni are not so organized or so empowered in the academic community as to be able to carry on the function of augmenting and preserving the financial resources of a college or university in the light of its composite educational objectives.

Educational Services

The quality of a college or university depends in the first instance upon the quality of its student input. Upholding the quality of student input is the function of an admissions program. The admission standards of a college or university are intimately connected with its academic objectives. For this reason the faculty has a very real concern with such standards. The number of students admitted and the general level of ability and interest evidenced by students are important issues for the entire academic community: faculty, students, alumni, and administration. As a rule, these policy issues may be determined by faculty and administration, subject to such external pressure or legal enactment as may influence college or university decision making.

The actual operation of an admissions program ordinarily falls to an administrative staff. Sometimes difficult individual cases may be referred to a faculty committee or even to a department or department chairman for consideration. But in general the admissions function has become a specialized service. The admissions officers must maintain close working relations with high school counselors, who have an increasingly important role in the identification of academic talent and in the channeling of students to particular colleges and universities. The admissions staff must interview prospective students and often, at the undergraduate level, their parents as well. Admissions officers must explain the academic objectives of the college or university and help students to fit their interests to those of the college or university. There are test score results, high school records, and letters of recommendations to collect and interpret for each admission applicant. Part of the task of counseling may be to suggest other colleges or universities, or even noncollege attendance. There are careful statistical calculations to make concerning the number of admissions in relation to the quantitative objectives of the college or university. There are admission applications to be correlated with student-aid needs. All this activity requires a large amount of talent devoted exclusively to its performance.

Another specialized function is that of course registration and student record keeping. The courses which a college or university offers through its various departments and other instructional units must be scheduled, and rooms must be assigned. Student enrollment must be recorded and academic achievement properly reported. Progress toward fulfillment of degree requirements must be observed. The completion of all requirements must be determined and the award of the appropriate degree must be arranged. A college or university must be prepared to certify a transcript of the official record of a student as needed for transfer or admission to another college or university or as desired for personnel files of an employer.

Furthermore, the previous academic record of a student in secondary school or in other colleges or universities is kept as a permanent record, along with any other items of personal evaluation besides course grades which a college or university may decide to maintain.

Student record keeping has become so voluminous and current operations so burdensome that the most modern techniques of record management are now essential in any sizable college or university. Thanks to present-day facilities in automatic data processing, student grade reports and cumulative grade-point averages can be completed in a matter of hours. The microfilming of past records is saving a great deal of storage space. New procedures in indexing and the machine recording of data make it possible to locate any file and report any transcript within minutes.

The importance of a library to the academic community is too well known to require any comment. There are some very real issues, however, to be resolved in library administration. Ideally, the library function is closely related to the academic objectives of a particular college or university. At the same time, library management has become a professional specialty in the academic community: The ordering, accessioning, cataloguing, custody, preservation, and distribution of books and periodicals must be carried out in an orderly, technical fashion. The work of helping students and scholars to use reference guides and to locate desired library materials relevant to a particular field or subject has also become a specialized activity. Moreover, the library facilities of a college or university must be operated some eighty to ninety or more hours a week. Ordinarily no other academic building on a college or university campus is so intensively used as a library.

Two major issues confront library management in a college or university today. One is the development of specialized library facilities. The concept of a central library building and central library operation is no longer accepted in most universities. It is recognized that a law school requires a special kind of library. Other professional schools have their peculiar library needs: medicine, architecture, music, art, journalism, among others. Furthermore, many departments and other professional schools desire that some library resources be as readily accessible as a laboratory. The problem then becomes one of how far a university shall go in establishing specialized library facilities and whether these special collections shall be centrally catalogued and controlled. Secondly, there is the question of how large a library collection a college or university should try to maintain. Shall every American book be purchased, and shall every American government paper be held? What past works shall be acquired? What foreign works shall be obtained? To what extent shall a library rely upon other libraries for assistance? What volumes shall be discarded or assigned to a central depository? How much can a college or university afford to spend for its library? How much space can a college or university afford to provide for its library?

These questions are academic matters, but they

are matters which library management must answer within the context of policy decisions representing a consensus of the faculty and administration of a college or university. Nor are these easy questions to answer. Increasingly, answers are being sought in terms of cooperation between colleges and universities, and this again means active administration leadership in building cooperative relations.

The library is no longer the only academic service needed on a college or university campus. To the extent desired, an audio-visual service may be established to prepare and to distribute charts, filmstrips, slides, and motion pictures to faculty members. More and more in recent years, perhaps in part encouraged by their training experience during World War II, faculty members have wanted specialized facilities and staff available to them in the preparation and presentation of visual and auditory materials. No longer is the lecture or discussion adequate with the instructor's words alone. And rather than draw his own crude graphic ideas on a blackboard, the scholar prefers to use technical assistance in handling visual materials.

Radio and television have become additional educational services. In some instances there is a tendency to look upon radio and television facilities as providing a kind of instructional laboratory of the speech department, or as providing an outlet for student activity. Radio and television are in fact an all-university instructional resource, a means of communication available to and valuable to every department. Perhaps some kinds of subject-matter materials are more readily adaptable to radio or television than others. Obviously music is especially appropriate for radio broadcast. But radio and television can be employed to present any subject matter, either as course material or as subject-matter elaboration or reinforcement.

Here again central administration is involved. A college or university cannot afford to have individual radio or television stations for every department or professional school. Transmission facilities are expensive and limited. They must be scheduled to their maximum usefulness and effectiveness.

In recent years in our large universities a new kind of central academic service has appeared, generally known as institutional research. Here the purpose has usually been to carry on studies concerned with the academic performance of the university: the utilization of academic space, the correlation of student performance with indications of student ability, the development of evidence of the quality achievements of students. Institutional research may also be used in the effort to develop norms for administrative use in the allocation of financial resources. Yet it seems to me that the essence of institutional research should be the learning process itself. After all, a first purpose of a college or university is the transmission of knowledge. Yet this process of learning is one of the little-known characteristics of human behavior. Today we spend great sums of money upon research in the various disciplines and professional fields of knowledge. Yet we often forget or overlook the need to devote some part of the resources of higher education

to inquiry into the process of learning itself and how
we may improve that process.

Image

Finally, I would say something about the image
of a college or university. Image is a word much with
us today, drawn from the lexicon of advertising into
common usage. Image means more than a statement
of purposes or objectives. Image embraces a whole
range of tangible and intangible factors which pro-
voke a public response. This response may determine
the ability of the academic community to realize its
avowed goals.

Each college or university must undertake to determine the image it desires to cultivate: the image of
academic excellence (there are various degrees of such
excellence), the image of student freedom and responsibility, the image of community service, the image of
athletic performance, the image of relationship to
various clientele and external groups, the image of
academic freedom. Words alone do not cultivate an
image. Actions are even more important.

Students help express an image. Faculty members help express an image. Alumni help express an
image. The kind of interest shown by the local community, the church, the state government, foundations, the federal government—all such interests help
express an image. And in the last analysis financial
support expresses an image.

There is a good deal of misunderstanding about
the term "quality," or "excellence," in an academic

community. It is sometimes assumed that only a college or university of a particular size can attain quality. It is sometimes assumed that only a particular kind of academic curriculum can indicate quality— a curriculum which emphasizes the disciplines rather than the professions. It is sometimes assumed that only an academic community with the same standards of performance for all undergraduate units and all graduate units can realize excellence. It is sometimes assumed that only privately sponsored colleges and universities can achieve quality. I would argue that none of these propositions is necessarily true.

The concept of service is another part of the image of a college or university. Service may be directed toward students, toward research, toward a local or church community, toward a particular profession. Service may be thought of as intended for a select group of students in terms of abilities and interests or for a diverse body of students. Service may be thought of in terms of broad social purpose, such as the provision of equality of educational opportunity, the development of intelligence among all social and economic classes, the promotion of an open society. In its community service a college or university is influenced by the economic and social characteristics of a particular locality. In its professional service and in other services a college or university may help part-time as well as full-time students. And of course a college or university may provide a general cultural service to a local community through public concerts, lectures, radio, and television.

The principal difficulty in constructing an image

of quality and service is the gulf which so often exists between aspiration and reality. Administrative officials are often tempted to cultivate an image for a particular college or university which is personally satisfying but completely unrealistic in terms of community need, available income, and prospective support. To many a scholar turned administrator, quality through a select student body and a rigorous curriculum is the only respectable image for a college or university. But this may not be the image which the community needs or which the faculty, student body, and alumni are willing to accept.

The issue here, however, is why administration should be considered the element of the academic community to develop and cultivate the image of a college or university. The answer is essentially one of elimination. Faculty members usually cannot or will not undertake the task. Faculty members are professionally oriented, concerned primarily with their particular discipline or professional field of knowledge. They are more closely tied to their colleagues in other colleges and universities who share their particular discipline than to their own local colleagues of other disciplines. Students come and go. Alumni are too busy in the practice of their profession and in the fulfillment of their local community obligations to have more than a partial, occasional interest in the image of their college or university.

As I have already commented, faculty, students, and alumni do contribute to the image of a particular college or university. Faculty members contribute with the work they do, the enthusiasm they evidence, the spirit they seek. Students contribute with the respect they acknowledge, the pride they develop, the growth they realize. Alumni contribute with the maturity they demonstrate, the support they provide, the concern for the values of education they honor.

But an image must be whole. It must be central to the purpose and the performance of an endeavor. It is the function of administration to try to see the academic community whole, as the sum which is greater than the component parts. It is the function of administration to hold that image high, to make it real, and to be sure that it is a realizable image. Administration because it is central must visualize the academic community in its entirety.

Perhaps the task of cultivating, developing, and expressing the image of a college or university falls upon the president more than upon anyone else. As an educational leader and as the chief administrative officer, the president is peculiarly situated to represent the college or university, to epitomize its image. No other single individual has so unique an opportunity, so heavy a responsibility. For this reason alone the selection of a president and the performance of a president are crucial to the operation of the academic community.

Chapter 7

Conflict and Consensus

A STRUGGLE for power is characteristic of all organized societies. There have been no known civilizations where a struggle for power did not occur in some form and in some degree. The static society may seek to avoid such a struggle by freezing the social relationship of all persons. The dynamic society experiences growth because struggle is an essential part of its existence. Toynbee presents struggle in civilization as conflict between a creative, dominant minority and an uncreative, acquiescent majority. And with prophetic insight he declares: "When leaders cease to lead, their tenure of power becomes an abuse." It is in a secession of the led from the leaders, it is in a loss of harmony among the parts which make up the whole "ensemble" of society that Toynbee finds the cause of the disintegration of a civilization.

However we may look upon a struggle for power —as a universal characteristic of society or as part of a dynamic process of growth and decline in civilization —that struggle is clearly evident in the recorded history of man as a political animal. The conservative looks upon man not simply as less than perfect but also as scarcely perfectible. He is willing to accept the faults of human beings as facts to which society must accommodate itself as best it can. The federal Constitution of our own nation accepts the struggle for power and endeavors to mitigate its tendency to tyrannical excess by a diffusion and limitation of power. The liberal looks upon men as equal in human dignity and in the sight of God and as somehow capable of growth in goodness through social progress. The Declaration of Independence insists that all men are created equal and endowed by their Creator with unalienable rights and that governments are instituted among men to secure these rights.

We are engaged nationally today in a great debate to decide whether power is essentially good, evil, or neutral. Some insist governmental power must be restricted because it is inherently evil, destructive of man's liberty from governmental control. Some argue that governmental power must be employed to advance social progress and that without such progress there can be no freedom for anyone in an organized society.

A considerable part of this controversy has slopped over into the academic community. Many persons seem to believe that American colleges and universities are composed only of scholars and students who seek to subvert the freedom of society through an expansion of governmental power, or even through a welcome to Soviet power. These critics do not know the academic community very well.

They are not aware of the variety of points of view which scholars and students consider, tentatively accept, and discard. They do not ask what contributions our colleges and universities make to the preservation of a creative minority in society or to the advancement of knowledge needed for national defense and social well-being. Indeed, a loss of public confidence in our institution of higher learning could be the surest act of subversion in American society which any group might manipulate. Moreover, these critics are often unaware of the struggle for power which goes on within the academic community.

Many scholars and students who appear to be willing to accept the idea of governmental power in society as a condition of social progress are equally or more emphatically opposed to administrative power as a condition of academic progress. They see such power only as an evil which calls for a redress. They, too, want power to be limited, or they want power to be redistributed and diffused.

This is one way of saying that there is conflict within the academic community, a conflict about power. Such conflict is evident, for example, in the "Statement of Principles of Faculty Participation in College and University Government" prepared by Committee T of the American Association of University Professors and published in the *Bulletin* of that association for the summer of 1960. I have no desire to criticize that statement of principles here. Beyond noting it as evidence of conflict, I shall observe only that the statement seems to accept the idea of hierarchy in college and university organization as opposed to the concept of community presented here. The existence of conflict is evident also in the numerous articles written by faculty members and others from time to time discussing the subject. I shall cite two as representative of a considerable literature.

A professor in a good, small college argues persuasively for faculty participation in the power structure of a college.[1] He insists that the role of administrators is to attend to the care and feeding of the college as a whole. He wants commitment and courage by administrators in making education and research their never-ceasing interest. In so far as trustees are concerned, he recognizes their role as legal custodians of the corporate nature of the college, but he tends to think of them, too, as an "oligarchy entrenched by self-perpetuation." Somehow the faculty member, we are told, feels trapped in an undemocratic world where his point of view has no voice. The faculty member, so it is said, has in his position "under the trustees" not even the equivalent power of a citizen who can vote, of a union member who can organize group forces, or of a shareholder who can demand an accounting.

Another faculty member turned dean is moved to comment about the growing tensions in the relationship of faculty and administration.[2] He believes the situation is more serious in our large universities.

[1] Arthur J. Dibden, "The Role of Administrators and Trustees: A Faculty View," *Association of American Colleges Bulletin,* vol. 44 (December, 1958), p. 536.

[2] Ben Euwema, "Academic Tensions," *The Educational Record,* vol. 42 (July, 1961), p. 187.

He cites as evidence the large number of dissatisfied faculty members and administrative officers who continually complain that the other group doesn't understand them. Administrators complain that faculty members don't take their duties seriously enough—in student advising, in preparation for classes, in attendance at university-wide functions. The faculty members blame administrators for low salaries, insufficient office space, inadequate facilities, an emphasis upon quantity rather than quality in student bodies, and a too ready response to external pressure.

The causes of these tensions are found in a failure to make complaints specific as to person and incident, in a failure to understand the complexities of administration on the one hand or the peculiarities of the academic performance on the other, and in a growing isolation of presidents from faculty members. The dean pleads for diversity of function within the community of scholars and bureaucrats.

In 1957 the American Council on Education sponsored a conference to discuss the nature and sources of faculty-administration tensions.[3] Here a university president and a university professor gave their "perspectives" on the subject. The then general secretary of the American Association of University Professors suggested "extending democratic processes" within colleges and universities. Yet he recognized also the dangers of too much committee work, of delays in decision making, and of a failure in responsi-

[3] Frank C. Abbott, *Faculty-Administration Relationships,* report of a work conference (Washington, D.C.: American Council on Education, 1958).

bility when faculties take on too many decisions. Others commented on the central problem from insights drawn from research in the behavioral sciences, from industrial organization, from labor relations, and from public administration.

Certainly no one can maintain that evidence of conflict is lacking within our academic communities. Instead, on all sides we are hearing more and more about the existence of such conflict.

Hierarchy and Conflict

Professor Victor A. Thompson has recently presented a theory of organizational conflict based upon hierarchical relationships.[4] His major proposition is that conflict arises between the specialization of persons in an organization and the authority of hierarchy. In any hierarchical pattern of personal relationships, there are positions in which individuals assume roles of either subordinates or superiors. Hierarchy, according to Professor Thompson, overemphasizes the power of veto and underemphasizes the reward of innovation. The superior expects obedience and loyalty from his subordinates. The superior expects deference. The superior is able to monopolize the means of communication in an organization. The superior usually has other powers: to select personnel, to determine organization, to initiate activities, to settle conflicts. Indeed, Thompson argues that the satisfac-

[4] Victor A. Thompson, "Hierarchy, Specialization, and Organizational Conflict," *Administrative Science Quarterly,* vol. 5 (March, 1961), p. 485.

tions of organizational life tend to be distributed by hierarchical rank.

On the other hand, the subordinate is more aware of his duties and obligations than of his power and rights. Professor Thompson declares that "the doctrines of democracy and liberalism which underlie our state have made almost no impact upon our bureaucratic organization." The subordinate tends to believe that his importance and dignity as an individual are hampered by his status in an organization. He feels that he may be undercompensated, deprived of deserved perquisites, subject to inconvenience in the performance of his work. The superior's power to restrict the subordinate's freedom of effort and to frustrate his ambitions results in latent or overt hostility.

Professor Thompson points out that the role of the superior, his behavior pattern in accordance with the expectations of others, has a strong charismatic element connected with it. The superior is expected to be superior in ability, talent, or performance. If he in fact fails to evidence such superiority, then conflict is more likely to occur. Furthermore, problem-solving procedures in an organization today require the combined efforts of many different specialists and technicians. Yet the personal as distinct from the organization purpose continues to be controlled by hierarchical relationships. It is the hierarchical system with its emphasis upon status and role which has appropriated the definition of success in our culture.

According to Professor Thompson there are four principal kinds of conflict within an organization.

The first arises from violation of role expectations. The superior expects a role of deference from sub-ordinates, but finds it difficult to obtain such deference; or the subordinate expects the superior to demonstrate his ability to evaluate his contribution properly but finds instead that the superior reveals an ignorance of the specialization. A second kind of conflict arises over the reality of interdependence among persons and groups. An individual is regarded as seeking unnecessarily to expand the jurisdiction of his activity in order to increase his status. Others see a threat to their status in such expansion. A third kind of conflict results from barriers to full and spontaneous communication throughout a hierarchy. The superior is considered no longer to desire frank advice and accurate knowledge. In the fourth place, conflict occurs when values and perceptions of reality in an organization are no longer shared by most people.

There is no need here to debate at length the theory that hierarchy as a pattern of personal interrelationships in an organization generates conflict. It appears that Professor Thompson has put forth a suggestive hypothesis indeed, if not a conclusive proposition. It may well be that hierarchy as a practice of organizational structure is inadequate to provide the kind of environment needed for certain types of cooperative effort among specialized talents.

I am personally disposed to believe that many situations of conflict which arise in an academic community are fundamentally conflicts about hierarchical relationships. The faculty member does not consider himself a subordinate of administration, of either the

president and his associates or the board of trustees.
Any attempt to introduce policies or practices which
suggest a role of superordination for the president on
one hand and a role of subordination for the professor
on the other hand will almost inevitably produce conflict.

A president who undertakes to decide who is
competent to teach a particular subject, who is competent to carry on research in some field, or how instruction or research shall be performed is assuming
a competency which usually he does not possess and
which others will not recognize. Any effort by a president to intervene in such matters poses a basic threat
to the very existence of a profession of scholarship. It
suggests that faculty members in the performance of
their instructional roles are subordinates of the president, subject to his direction and supervision.

Many conflicts about academic freedom in a college or university are actually conflicts about a real or
imagined hierarchical relationship. A president or a
board of trustees may find objectionable some activity on the part of a professor which outrages popular
sensibilities. Such activity usually occurs not in the
classroom but in a public gathering or in public me-
dia of communication. Let us pass by any examples in
the realm of what constitutes advocacy of collectivism
or even subversion. Instead, let us use two other illus-
trations.

Let us imagine that a faculty member writes a
letter to a newspaper and endorses the proposition
that only the top 10 per cent of college-age youth
should be admitted to college, and that these should

be selected exclusively on the basis of a rigorous standardized test administered on a national basis. Although such a proposition lacks the emotional excitement of a resolution to abolish the House Un-American Activities Committee or to recognize Communist China, it certainly does violence to the entrenched attitudes of an important and vocal segment of the American public. A president and a board of trustees will certainly hear about so outrageous a point of view and will be asked what they intend to do about it.

Or let us imagine a case where a faculty member appears in a public gathering of students and parents and advocates that college students be encouraged to experiment with sexual intercourse as a means to physical and emotional maturity. Parents, religious leaders, newspaper editors, and many others—perhaps even some students—will denounce such a point of view vigorously and demand that a president and board of trustees take immediate action to prevent the faculty member from saying such a thing again. If the university is dependent upon public appropriations, its very sustenance may be threatened.

For the present we can ignore the difficult issue of just what constitutes academic freedom in the academic community and what are the absolutely minimum essentials for its preservation. My point is that when faculty members make public statements which arouse the ire of an influential and vocal element of the public, and when critics demand that a college or university punish the offending speaker, the immediate and pressing issue is one of hierarchy. It is assumed by the outside critics that a university is a pattern of superior and subordinate relationships. The president and the board of trustees are the superiors. The professor is the subordinate. If the superior does not repudiate the offending subordinate, if the superior does not chastise the subordinate, then he is accepting his point of view.

On the other hand, faculty members look at the episode from an entirely different perspective. Few if any will agree with the public statement of their colleague. But they will immediately perceive a threat to the status of all if the power of president and board to take disciplinary action is accepted without protest. To the external world the issue may seem to be one of equality of educational opportunity or one of common morality. The faculty as a group and the college or university as an entity are pictured as condoning questionable points of view. Within the academic community the issue is seen entirely as one of organizational relationships. The question of superordination and subordination within the academic community is never perceived by the public at large.

I have already expressed my own point of view in so far as the organization of a college or university is concerned. I do not believe that the concept of hierarchy is a realistic representation of the interpersonal relationships which exist within a college or university. Nor do I believe that a structure of hierarchy is a desirable prescription for the organization of a college or university.

The concept of hierarchy may be a useful tool of analysis in the study of group and individual behavior within formal social groups. The difficulty with such a tool of analysis is that many persons may come to assume that hierarchy is being advocated as the desirable system of structural relationships. More than this, hierarchy is apt to be considered the only possible relationship among people grouped together in a common, purposeful enterprise.

I would argue that there is another concept of organization just as valuable as a tool of analysis and even more useful as a generalized observation of group and interpersonal behavior. This is the concept of community. It is the concept of community which I have applied to the description of college and university organization presented herein. To how many different kinds of groups the concept of community may be applicable, I am not prepared to say. That it is applicable to our colleges and universities seems to me clearly evident.

The concept of community presupposes an organization in which functions are differentiated and in which specializations must be brought together in a harmonious whole. But this process of bringing together, of coordination if you will, is achieved not through a structure of superordination and subordination of persons and groups but through a dynamic of consensus.

It seems somewhat surprising that a concept of community should have received so little consideration in the United States as a theory of organization. Certainly it is a concept of community rather than of hierarchy which characterizes the system of governmental power in our country. Writing in support of the newly drafted federal constitution, James Madison declared (*The Federalist,* no. 47): "No political truth is . . . of greater intrinsic value . . . than that . . . the accumulation of all powers, legislative, executive and judiciary, in the same hands whether of one, a few, or many, and whether hereditary, self-appointed, or elective, may justly be pronounced the very definition of tyranny."

In the political and governmental life of the United States we have sought to avoid despotism by a limitation of power and a distribution or sharing of power. There is no concept of hierarchy in the political structure of our society. The system of political parties is organized on the basis of local units of power. These local units are gathered into a community which is the state political party, and the state units into a community which is the national political party. The political party operates on the basis of consensus. In turn, the governmental system is organized on the basis of a distribution of power among legislative, executive, and judicial branches and a distribution of power between a federal government and state governments. This is not a hierarchy of power but rather a system of community of interest which operates through a practice of consensus.

Accordingly, the idea of a community rather than a hierarchy of power is not strange to Americans. Government has long exemplified such a concept, and even subject to the heavy strains of two world wars, economic depression, and the competition of Communist imperialism our governmental system has retained considerable vigor. The idea of community as the basis for organization of our colleges and universities should not then seem remarkable.

The concept of hierarchy may be appropriate for our military forces, at least within the military departments, if not within the Department of Defense itself. The concept of hierarchy may be appropriate for our business corporations, although it may be in fact less valid than is often presupposed as a result of the emergence of union power and the growth of research and development as a basic force in business growth and survival. The concept of hierarchy may be appropriate to some administrative activities of government, even if it is less evident than many seem to think.

The only justification I can find for the idea of hierarchy in a college or university is the formal, legal authority of boards of trustees to "govern" the academic community.[5] It is sometimes thought that the board of trustees as an organizational device is a peculiar American invention. Professor W. H. Cowley points out that while boards of trustees were unknown to Oxford and Cambridge, a board did exist at the University of Leyden in the Netherlands, where the

[5] I am concerned with the organization of a college or university as a secular body. I have no desire to invade the realm of church organization in this discussion. I am tempted to observe that where rules or traditions of church organization supersede the traditions of the academic community within a church-related college or university, the purposes of the church have taken precedence over the purpose of higher education. It is my observation that in practice the leading church-related colleges and universities in America tend in their organizational practice to reflect academic traditions more than their particular church traditions.

idea had come from the Italian universities, and at the University of Edinburgh, whence it apparently was exported to both Yale and Princeton in colonial America.[6] Just how extensive was the authority of such boards in the eighteenth century only a careful study could establish. It does seem evident, however, that the American board of trustees was not without some European precedent.

The statement on faculty participation in college and university government by Committee T of the American Association of University Professors suggests that boards of trustees were given control of colleges and universities because for many years there was no considerable body of "professional scholars of repute" to whom authority could be entrusted. It is true that only in the past century, and more particularly in the last sixty years, have a goodly number of professional scholars characterized the faculties of our leading colleges and universities.[7] The committee then acknowledges that a "functional sharing of powers" has been realized within a framework which appears to "ordain a concentration of powers."

[6] I have had the advantage of reading an unpublished manuscript by Professor Cowley of Stanford University. See W. H. Cowley, "Academic Government," *Educational Forum*, vol. 15 (January, 1951), p. 217; and W. H. Cowley, "The Government and Administration of Higher Education: Whence and Whither," *Journal of the American Association of Collegiate Registrars*, vol. 22 (July, 1947), p. 477.

[7] W. H. Cowley, "College and University Teaching, 1858–1958," in Russell M. Cooper, ed., *The Two Ends of the Log: Learning and Teaching in Today's College* (Minneapolis: University of Minnesota Press, 1958), p. 101.

Regardless of apparent prescription, it seems fairly clear that in practice boards of trustees do not exercise an absolute, or hierarchical, authority within most colleges and universities—certainly not in the larger and leading colleges and universities. Power is shared by the major constituent elements of the academic community. I have already endeavored to describe this power structure. A great many persons have sensed this situation without clearly or concisely proclaiming it.

After speaking of a "functional sharing of power," Committee T of the American Association of University Professors proposes as its first principle of academic government not just faculty representation at "each major organizational level" of a college or university but also direct communication between the faculty and the board of trustees which is not dependent upon "the chief administrative officers." Presumably these chief administrative officers are the dean of a college and the provost or vice president for academic affairs of a university, together with the president. The statement of principles by Committee T does not make clear why this arrangement of direct communication is desirable.

One of two factors, or perhaps both, may explain the position of Committee T. One possibility is that faculty members do in practice think of academic organization as a hierarchy of power. If it is conceded that boards of trustees do in practice determine fundamental issues of academic policy, program, and practice, then faculty representation may be warranted. Yet surely the cause of faculty representation within or before the board of trustees is purchased at a high price if it is obtained at the cost of acknowledging board authority on an extensive scale in matters academic.

The other possible explanation of faculty attitude toward representation on the board of trustees is that faculty members do not regard the dean or provost and the president as faculty representatives. This is an unfortunate situation. A dean or a provost and the president of a college or university have a dual role. They are faculty officers as well as administrative officers. The insistence that faculty members should be consulted in the appointment of department chairmen, deans, a provost (or vice president), and a president is surely based upon the fundamental proposition that all of these are faculty positions. Such consultation seems to me both reasonable and essential. Where consultation does not take place, the faculty role of chairmen, deans, provosts, and presidents is seriously compromised. The president's position as an administrative officer is also jeopardized under these circumstances.

As officers of the faculty, a dean of a college or the provost of a university and the president are expected to present the faculty point of view to a board of trustees on those matters where academic power and administrative power overlap. When a faculty in its collective capacity demands separate representation before the board, it is voicing a vote of no confidence in its dean and president. Under such circumstances, a dean and president have no honorable course of action open to them except to resign and propose that the board designate faculty leaders who do or will enjoy the confidence of the faculty in its collective capacity. It is difficult to see how a dean and president can function effectively without faculty as well as board confidence.

Furthermore, a dean and president will in ordinary circumstances communicate board decisions to the faculty, especially where these decisions directly affect academic affairs. Any matter of faculty interest or inquiry is worth careful and full communication by the administration. Where faculty points of view are expressed, these should be known to a board of trustees as well as to the president. Where there are differences, consensus between faculty and administration is essential. The president is the avenue for negotiating such consensus.

As I have commented earlier, many faculty members appear to be dissatisfied with a system of government which leaves the selection of faculty leaders to a process of appointment, with consultation, rather than a process of direct election. The proposal for direct communication to the board of trustees from the faculty through representatives of its own choosing is in reality a proposal for direct election of faculty leaders. Where in a few instances of faculty representation on boards of trustees actual conflict has not resulted, it seems to be largely because the elected faculty representatives have refused to become faculty leaders. Instead, such faculty members have tended to let presidents and their associates speak for the faculty and have simply confirmed to the board that the president does in fact fairly represent faculty points of view.

In a study made a short time ago by a distinguished corporation executive, a good deal of attention was given to this question of faculty representation on a board of trustees other than through the president and his academic associates. The conclusion was set forth in these words: "That a faculty representative should be present to argue with the president, or even as a 'watch-dog' to report the president's performance back to the faculty, is clearly contrary to all principles of good organization." [8] Mr. Belcher did not make clear exactly what these principles were. Earlier, however, he had identified three "primary decision-making groups" in the university, and it seems reasonable to suppose that he was thinking in terms of organizational principles applicable to an academic community and not simply of those applicable in the hierarchy of a business corporation.

If the concept of community rather than of hierarchy is to be accepted as the basis of organization of a college or university, then the various organizational arrangements for the conduct of all affairs of the college or university should be consistent with this concept. Consciously or unconsciously, those who discuss college or university organization, even when they dimly perceive the reality of community, often lapse into use of the concept of hierarchy to describe existing or to prescribe desirable relationships. The con-

[8] Donald R. Belcher, *The Board of Trustees of the University of Pennsylvania,* a report of the Educational Survey of the University of Pennsylvania (Philadelphia: University of Pennsylvania Press, 1960), p. 44.

cept of community as opposed to the concept of hierarchy in our colleges and universities will become real in discussion, as it tends to be in practice, only when discussion proceeds from that premise.

Community and Conflict

If we accept the proposition that much conflict within our colleges and universities stems from efforts by some element or other to impose a concept of hierarchy upon the academic community, we may assume that the concept of community would substantially lessen conflict. Where conflict does not characterize a college or university—at least conflict in any virulent and overt sense—I believe the practice of community will generally be found to prevail. Otherwise, it may be expected that the faculty is not a company of professional scholars.

But the concept of community is not an automatic guarantee that there will be consensus rather than conflict. I am disposed to believe that conflict may be less bitter when it is confined to the merits of a particular issue rather than when it embraces far-reaching questions of power as well as substance. Yet it is naïve indeed to suppose that conflict within the academic community can be eliminated by some magic organizational formula. Conflict may always be expected when individuals work together.

Conflict is not necessarily an undesirable state of affairs. The late Mary Parker Follett once wrote a little essay with the intriguing title "Constructive

Conflict." [9] She made the point that conflict reveals the existence of differing interests and differing attitudes. Conflict defines differences. But conflict is constructive only when it gives way to action by all parties involved. Miss Follett identified three methods of dealing with conflict: (1) domination, (2) compromise, and (3) integration. The third method was the one which made conflict constructive. Instead of the word "integration," I prefer the term "consensus."

In a system of shared power, conflict may surely be expected. It is too much to expect that different persons and differing groups who wield power will want to collaborate willingly and readily. Necessity, however, may produce a reluctant if nonetheless definite consensus. In a system of shared power, conflict means frustration of power, a mutual cancellation of purpose and accomplishment, unless conflict becomes consensus. Conflict can result in a state of nihilism. Conflict may also give way to consensus by which those who share power unite to realize shared purpose. In the United States we have been fortunate in being able to keep conflict within limits and in moving from conflict to consensus. The American political system operates in this way. The American institution of higher education does also.

I know of no way to guarantee that organization based upon a concept of community will necessarily achieve action based upon consensus. I can only ob-

[9] Henry C. Metcalf and L. Urwick, *Dynamic Administration: The Collected Papers of Mary Parker Follett* (New York: Harper & Brothers, 1941), p. 30.

serve that consensus has in fact been realized by most colleges and universities. There can be and is conflict among the constituent elements of the academic community. But much of the time such conflict gives way in practice to tacit or explicit consensus. When consensus is not possible, then new leadership is usually needed.

It is impossible here to survey the range of issues which result in conflict within the academic community. This is an essay on organization rather than a study of conflict. Needless to say, there are many problems in quality of educational endeavor, programs of service, curricula, instructional methods, student behavior, alumni requests, financial support, among others, which agitate the academic community almost continuously. In varying ways these problems are resolved by colleges and universities. In some instances there is no such thing as a satisfactory solution; often the constituent elements of the academic community must simply learn to live with their problems.

It may be useful for our purposes, however, to discuss two particular problems as illustrative of the organizational relationships which are involved within the academic community. I select these two problems from many because they are important in and of themselves, and because they provide an especially useful illustration of both conflict and consensus. One of these problems is that of utilization of the financial resources of a college or university. The other problem is that of professional ethics to guide the individual conduct of faculty members and administrative officials.

Institutional Resources

Apart from conflict about organizational arrangements as such, there is probably no substantive issue in a college or university which tends to divide a faculty from administration as does the issue of utilization of financial resources. As I have observed before, no college or university in the United States considers itself to have sufficient current operating income for all its immediate needs. The budget process is therefore one of dividing up limited resources among competing demands.

The problems of income utilization are numerous indeed within a college or university. The larger a university is in terms of numbers of students and scope of instructional and research programs, the larger will be the corresponding income. The larger the university, the greater the variety of specializations which tend to arise. The larger the university, the greater the various services which the university may be expected to render to the faculty. The available income never seems sufficient to meet all these needs.

In our discussion here we shall confine our attention to educational and general expenditures. We might include some mention of auxiliary services and student aid, because these are important activities and because they may on occasion (as with student aid) drain off general income which might otherwise be available for educational purposes. It is sufficient, however, for our purpose to restrict our comments to that broad category of current activity which is generally labeled "educational and general." The component elements of educational expenditure may be classified in terms of objects (personal services, equipment, supplies, and operations) and they may be classified in terms of broad purpose. The standard classifications of purpose are departmental instruction, "organized" or separately budgeted research, extension and public service, libraries, organized activities related to instructional departments, plant operation and maintenance, and administration and general.

Once these classifications are established they present a particular pattern for an individual college or university. This pattern may vary over a period of years as influenced by various internal events. If a university, for example, acquires a medical school, a goodly portion of its income may henceforth be required with which to operate a teaching hospital. This increases expenditures under the heading "organized activities related to instructional departments." And inevitably the pattern of expenditure at one particular college or university will be compared with that of another, even though numerous studies show that there is no such thing as a standard or uniform expenditure pattern among colleges and universities.[10]

[10] See, for example, National Federation of College and University Business Officers Associations, *A Study of Income and Expenditures in Sixty Colleges—Year 1953–1954* (1955); and *California and Western Conference Cost and Statistical Study for the Year 1954–1955* (Berkeley, Calif.: University of California Press, 1959).

Administrative officers have been somewhat restive in the use of the sevenfold classification just mentioned, since they believe it tends to lodge too large a proportion of total expenditures within the single category "administration and general." As a result, three additional categories are often utilized. These are student personnel services, general institutional expense, and staff benefits. In some cases staff benefits have been distributed among various purposes as an additional item of compensation for personal services.

Although general definitions have been provided for the seven or ten principal categories of educational expense, there is a good deal of variety in the actual classification of expenditures by individual colleges and universities. This is one of the reasons why it is so difficult to compare patterns of expenditure among colleges and universities. For this same reason expenditure analysis is frequently misleading. For example, should a laboratory school used as an adjunct to the program of teacher education be included as a cost of instruction or as an organized activity related to instructional departments? Is an audio-visual service engaged in providing service to instructional departments to be classified as instructional expense or general institutional expense? Should the costs of a departmental or school library (such as a law school library) be considered part of instructional or library expense? Should the expense of telephone service in faculty offices be included in instructional costs or general institutional costs? Such questions can be continued in large number. Different answers necessarily provide different results in the educational and general expenditure of a college or university.

Two kinds of criticism often arise from within a faculty about the expenditure pattern of a college or university. First, there may be some disposition on the part of certain departments and schools to question the instructional costs of other departments and schools. Any university with a medical school has undertaken a very high cost program of instruction. Unless there is a special endowment for operation of the medical school, some faculty members may believe that a disproportionately large part of general income is being channeled into medical education. In a college, a department of English or of government, for example, may be critical of the large equipment and supply expenditures budgeted to a department of chemistry or physics. In addition to this kind of complaint, faculty members are likely to believe that expenditures for plant operation, for general institutional purposes, for student services, and for administration are too large.

Oftentimes a college or university faculty overlooks or does not know the extent of the items which are covered by these college and university-wide categories of expenditure. Thus, it may be customary to include under the heading of general institutional expense such items as telephone service for the whole college or university, all travel costs of faculty as well as of administrative staff, all postal expenditure, all mimeograph service, all staff benefits, all entertainment costs for guests, all concerts and lectures, all commencement and convocation expenses, all membership fees in educational and learned societies, all subsidy of faculty publications, and publication of catalogues and bulletins. Many of these items of expenditure are of direct benefit to faculty members. Yet because they are labeled "general institutional expense" there is a tendency on the part of faculty members to think that the whole category of outlay is unduly large and wasteful. To the faculty an outlay is hard to justify unless it is for instruction as such.

There may be some reason on occasion why college and university faculty members believe as they do. There may indeed be waste or extravagant expenditure for plant maintenance, for general institutional expense, and for administration. Every category of college or university expenditure requires constant and critical consideration. Moreover, self-conscious as college and university faculties are about the general level of academic salaries, there is a kind of continuing expectation these days that income will be allocated each year in such a way as to bring about some improvement in salary levels.[11] If this expectation is not fulfilled, there is a real concern about other items of college and university expenditure.

It is not enough for administrative officers and boards to argue that the faculty itself can do much to improve levels of faculty compensation.[12] All such

[11] See Sidney G. Tickton, *Teaching Salaries Then and Now—A Second Look* (New York: The Fund for the Advancement of Education, 1961).

[12] As was argued in Beardsley Ruml and Donald H. Morrison, *Memo to a College Trustee* (New York: McGraw-Hill Book Company, Inc., 1959).

schemes inevitably involve an increase in the student-faculty ratio or an economy in direct instructional outlays. These adjustments will usually be accepted only upon a clear conviction that other operating economies in a college or university are not equally available.

The problem then in constructing an operating budget for a college or university is one of achieving some degree of consensus about the utilization of income between faculty and administration. To be sure, administration bears the final authority and responsibility for budget decisions. But a faculty is rightly interested in and entitled to some participation in this decision making.

One of the critical concerns of the university community in recent years has been how to achieve the desirable degree of faculty participation in budget making. There is, of course, no question about the fact that departments must be consulted about their expenditure needs. The budget process starts at the departmental level. Some discretion may be given to a department or school in deciding its staffing level, its general distribution of staff by ranks, and its equipment and supply requirements. The department chairman or a departmental committee has the major burden of evaluating faculty service and of proposing relative salary increases. All this is normal budget routine in many colleges and universities.

The real task is one of weighing the relative merits of increased demands among instructional units such as the school of medicine, the school of agriculture, the school of engineering, the school of education, and the college of arts and sciences. And in turn the instructional costs of all departments and schools must be judged in the light of library, organized activity, plant operation, student personnel, general expense, and administration needs. How is a faculty to know and evaluate all these other demands upon the income of the college and university?

In a few instances, apparently, a college or university has a formal budget committee of faculty members in which these problems of budget making are fully discussed by administration officials. There can be no objection, I feel, to such a practice, although it is certainly time-consuming and can in the long run add further cost to the operation of a college or university. The least that can be done, I believe, is to publish the budget in some kind of summary form for faculty information. This implies a readiness for administration to answer questions about the various items of expenditure.

In any event, in some way the academic community needs to achieve consensus about the utilization of the financial resources of a college or university for current operating purposes.

Professional Ethics

Let me say again that education, like religion, seeks to achieve an ordered change in man's behavior. By increasing the store of knowledge, by transmitting the accumulated ideas of the past, by promoting skill in the use of knowledge, education seeks to promote the abilities of man to improve his material and intellectual well-being. If the purpose of education were purely esoteric, the cultivation of knowledge for its own sake; if the purpose of higher education were unrelated to the everyday life of our culture; then education could be an adornment and a luxury of society.

Because Americans expect education to be useful, we have made it a cause for concern. Education can be useful only if it is given practical application in business, professions, government, and other social institutions. Education can be useful only if advancing knowledge results in improvement in social endeavor. It is little wonder that professional scholars embrace the idea of progress. They would be impractical men indeed if they did not do so.

It appears that in the United States we live in a time when change is particularly confusing, when change seems to threaten the security of large numbers of individuals. Depression and recession have undermined confidence in economic growth and maximum employment through the natural law of the market place. World War II compelled the United States to become a major power and the reluctant leader of Western culture. The challenge of communism as a philosophy of life and as a competitive culture has brought into question the power of our own philosophy of life and culture.

There have been other reasons for anxiety. Inflation has threatened the adequacy of fixed incomes. Unemployment and low incomes have threatened the material well-being of large numbers of unskilled marginal laborers, urban and rural alike. High taxes have discouraged the accumulation of wealth by some. Slums have discouraged the prospect of improved living for others. Scientific research and technological development have proceeded so rapidly that few have been able to understand either. New scientific theories and new social concepts have exceeded the intellectual grasp of large numbers of people. And a rapidly growing population has presented new challenges in education, transportation, housing, and care of the aged.

In an age of social anxiety and frustration, there are many different forms of response. Toynbee has identified various stages in the breakdown of a civilization and various attempts at a slowing down or reversal of such breakdown. He insists that there is no basis in history for deterministic theories of the decline and fall of a civilization, such as a "running down" of the universe, or a given life span, or a deterioration in the quality of individuals. He rejects any cyclical pattern in human events or a theory of loss of command over a particular environment. Toynbee insists that breakdowns occur because of social conflict and schism, evident in a tendency to idolize a society or national group, in a tendency to idolize a particular technique or social process, in a tendency to idolize the past ("archaism"), in a tendency to defeatism and drift, in a tendency to loss of self-discipline and integrity, and in a tendency to escape from the present into an imagined utopia of the future.

Toynbee does not venture to determine whether Western civilization is in a period of growth or breakdown. Since he rejects any idea of determinism, he believes that it is not beyond man's power to influence the fate of the future of Western society, provided men exercise the powers of individual creativity. These propositions of Toynbee may or may not be acceptable to historical scholars or others.

Our interest here is in a simple fact. Education is committed to an assumption of growth and creativity. It rejects any assumption of inevitable breakdown. But beyond this fact, we are confronted with an equal fact: that we have no basis in knowledge for outlining or planning a sure course of growth in human affairs. Just as there may be no determinism in social collapse, there may be no determinism in social improvement.

In this state of social confusion and limited knowledge, education finds itself in a particularly vulnerable position. This is especially true of higher education, concerned as it is with the wider reaches of man's intellectual capacity. On the one hand, higher education is committed to social growth and progress through the improvement of man's mind and skill. On the other hand, higher education cannot provide any certain prediction of the path to social growth and progress. With those who oppose the idea of growth and progress, higher education finds no basis of agreement. For those who embrace the idea of growth and progress, higher education offers nc certain knowledge; it offers only a faith and a procedure of tentative, cautious experimentation.

The problem of ethics within the academic community is one of formulating a code of scholarly behavior which makes clear both the commitments and the limitations of higher education. To be sure, higher education can function as we know it today in Western society only if society values and preserves freedom. In a different society, no doubt, the institution of higher education would have different commitments and different procedures. This interrelation of society and institutional characteristics is another part of the problem of ethics.

Today in our country higher education is under attack fundamentally from two points of view. First, there are those whose anxieties and frustrations lead them to question the idea of social growth and progress. They are fearful of change. Secondly, there are those who expect knowledge to offer sure solutions to social ills and who suspect failure of effort or alienation of loyalty when higher education admits its limitations.

Administration is troubled when these criticisms threaten the very existence of a college or university. Administrative officials are concerned to maintain the integrity and the good repute of the academic community. Scholars share this concern. Conflict arises when administrative officials feel that scholars have not observed an appropriate restraint in their presentation of the scope and reliability of knowledge. Conflict also arises when scholars feel that administrative officers have not observed an appropriate commitment to the assumption of social growth and progress through the free discussion of varied ideas.

There is a great need in higher education for a code of ethics for faculty and administration which will define standards of behavior for both. Even more, there is a need for instruments of action which can police extremes of behavior which threaten academic responsibility or academic freedom. Unfortunately, faculties have been reluctant to assert their professional duty to establish and enforce standards of ethical behavior, and administrative officials have often been more interested in the behavioral lapses of scholars than in their own.

Here is a particularly fruitful area for consensus within the academic community. Nor can the effort to achieve such consensus be long delayed. The present uneasy and tacit agreement between administrative officials and scholars to observe academic responsibility and to uphold academic freedom is subject to breakdown under stress. It would be helpful indeed if a code of ethics for the entire academic community could be formulated and observed with some care.

Contributors to Consensus

All the constituent elements of the academic community—faculty, students, alumni, and administration—must be united in good will if consensus is to be achieved. Shared power can be preserved only in a society of shared respect.

The academic community as an organizational structure is a system of shared power. At the same time a college or a university is a community with common needs, common commitments, and common aspirations. There is no necessity in the academic community for that degree of precise coordination of effort which may be required in a large industrial establishment or in a military force. The objective of higher education is realized in the minds and actions of individual students, as inspired by scholars and as influenced by the academic environment. The advancement of knowledge through either the collection of facts or their interpretation must be achieved by individual scholars, or occasionally by teams of scholars and assistants.

The faculty of a college or university is a company of scholars with individual and collective authority and responsibility. Instruction and research is first of all personal. The selection of members of the faculty, the determination of course offerings and instructional practices, the rank of faculty members, the establishment of degree requirements—all these are collective responsibilities of a faculty exercised at the departmental, the college or school, and the university level. Evaluation of student performance and of student fulfillment of degree requirements is performed by individual faculty members or by faculty committees.

At each level of collective faculty authority some leadership is necessary. At the departmental level the chairman is the nominal leader. At the school or college level the dean is the nominal leader. At the university level the president and the provost constitute a joint team of leadership. To be sure, this is not a structure of elected leadership, although influential faculty members are almost always consulted about the appointment of any individual to each such position. But such leadership is not authoritarian either.

It operates through formal voting or common agreement of all faculty members or their representatives.

This structure of academic leadership has one great advantage for the realization of consensus within the academic community. Such a leadership structure of deans and a president is intimately related to the structure of administration within a college or especially a university. The president, I repeat, is both an academic leader and a chief administrative officer. He occupies a unique position to promote consensus between faculty and administration. When there is a breakdown in consensus there is almost always an accompanying breakdown in leadership.

The role of students and alumni in the academic community is somewhat different from that of faculty and administration. Students are influential in large measure to the extent that they accept and promote the educational objectives of a particular college or university. If students are often preoccupied with other concerns than academic achievement, this fact is revealed in tension and even conflict within the academic community. The student element is one no college or university can ignore, even if the relations of faculty and administration with students are at times troublesome. As former students, alumni are also influential. Here again there may be conflict about the educational objectives of the academic community.

The student personnel staff of a college or university labors valiantly to help build consensus between students, faculty, and administration. Directors of alumni relations and other administrative officials, including deans and presidents, seek to promote consensus among alumni, faculty, students, and administration. In most instances substantial achievement is realized from these various endeavors.

The academic community abhors absolute power. It is committed to freedom through a sharing of power. Consensus in action is the test of both freedom and responsibility. Such consensus is essential to make the American college and university the exciting, indispensable force it is for the preservation of growth and creativity in our Western civilization.

Index

261

Gardner, John W., 161
Gerth, H. H., 8n.
Gordon, Robert A., 29n.
Government and higher
education, 49–53
Gray, Ailsa P., 23n.
Gulick, Luther, 11n., 15

Hardy, C. DeWitt, 37n.,
125n.
Harris, Seymour E., 45n.,
47, 48, 127n.
Harvard University, 37,
151
Heady, Ferrel, 10n.
Henderson, Algo D., 165n.
Hierarchy of authority, 23–
26, 31, 63–64, 181,
229–235
Higher education, excel-
lence in, 161–163
financing, 44–49, 115–
120, 209–214, 246–
252
government and, 49–53
as an institution, 5, 33–
64
as an organization, 25–
27, 31, 58–64
religion and, 35–40
welfare and, 40–43
Hofstadter, Richard, 37,
38n., 57, 125n.
Holden, Paul E., 11n.

Hollinshead, Byron S.,
129n.
Howell, James E., 29n.
Hughes, Raymond M.,
182n.
Hutchins, Robert M., 90

Indiana University, 152
Institutional research, 219–
220

Jacob, Philip E., 142, 143
Janowitz, Morris, 66n.
Johns Hopkins University,
152

Keeney, Barnaby C., 128n.
Keezer, Dexter M., 45n.
Kirk, Russell, 57n.

Lazarsfeld, Paul F., 67n.
Library, 216–218
Litchfield, Edward H., 8,
21n., 100n.
Lloyd-Jones, Esther, 203n.
Long, John D., 195n.
Loyalty to colleges and uni-
versities, 167–172
Luther, Martin, 36

McGee, Reece J., 67n.
McGrath, Earl J., 126n.
MacIver, Robert M., 57n.